Teaching Child Management Skills

Pergamon Titles of Related Interest

Cartledge/Milburn TEACHING SOCIAL SKILLS TO CHILDREN:
Innovative Approaches, Second Edition
Eisenson LANGUAGE AND SPEECH DISORDERS IN CHILDREN
Johnson/Rasbury/Siegel APPROACHES TO CHILD TREATMENT:
Introduction to Theory, Research and Practice
Kirby/Grimley UNDERSTANDING AND TREATING ATTENTION
DEFICIT DISORDER
Morris/Kratochwill THE PRACTICE OF CHILD THERAPY
Pope/McHale/Craighead SELF-ESTEEM ENHANCEMENT WITH
CHILDREN AND ADOLESCENTS
Santostefano COGNITIVE CONTROL THERAPY WITH CHILDREN
AND ADOLESCENTS
Schwartz/Johnson PSYCHOPATHOLOGY OF CHILDHOOD:
A Clinical-Experimental Approach, Second Edition

Related Journals*

CLINICAL PSYCHOLOGY REVIEW
JOURNAL OF CHILD PSYCHOLOGY AND PSYCHIATRY

*Free sample copies available upon request

PSYCHOLOGY PRACTITIONER GUIDEBOOKS
EDITORS
Arnold P. Goldstein, Syracuse University
Leonard Krasner, Stanford University & SUNY at Stony Brook
Sol L. Garfield, Washington University

Teaching Child Management Skills

RICHARD F. DANGEL

and

RICHARD A. POLSTER
The University of Texas at Arlington

HQ
755.7
.D36
1988
WEST

PERGAMON PRESS
New York · Oxford · Beijing · Frankfurt
São Paulo · Sydney · Tokyo · Toronto

U.S.A.	Pergamon Press, Maxwell House, Fairview Park, Elmsford, New York 10523, U.S.A.
U.K.	Pergamon Press, Headington Hill Hall, Oxford OX3 0BW, England
PEOPLE'S REPUBLIC OF CHINA	Pergamon Press, Room 4037, Qianmen Hotel, Beijing, People's Republic of China
FEDERAL REPUBLIC OF GERMANY	Pergamon Press, Hammerweg 6, D-6242 Kronberg, Federal Republic of Germany
BRAZIL	Pergamon Editora, Rua Eça de Queiros, 346, CEP 04011, Paraiso, São Paulo, Brazil
AUSTRALIA	Pergamon Press Australia, P.O. Box 544, Potts Point, N.S.W. 2011, Australia
JAPAN	Pergamon Press, 8th Floor, Matsuoka Central Building, 1-7-1 Nishishinjuku, Shinjuku-ku, Tokyo 160, Japan
CANADA	Pergamon Press Canada, Suite No. 271, 253 College Street, Toronto, Ontario, Canada M5T 1R5

Copyright © 1988 Pergamon Books Inc.

All Rights Reserved. No part of this publication may be reproduced, stored in a retrieval system or transmitted in any form or by any means: electronic, electrostatic, magnetic tape, mechanical, photocopying, recording or otherwise, without permission in writing from the publishers.

First edition 1988

Library of Congress Cataloging-in-Publication Data
Dangel, Richard F.
Teaching child management skills.
(Psychology practitioner guidebooks)
Bibliography: p.
Includes index.
1. Parenting — Study and teaching — United States.
2. Behavior modification — Study and teaching — United States. I. Polster, Richard A. II. Title. III. Series.
[DNLM: 1. Behavior Therapy — methods. 2. Child Behavior Disorders — therapy. 3. Parent-Child Relation. 4. Teaching — methods. WS350.6 D182t]
HQ755.7.D36   1988   649'.1'07   87-14721

British Library Cataloguing in Publication Data
Dangel, Richard F.
Teaching child management skills. —
(Psychology practitioner guidebooks).
1. Behavior therapy.   2. Child psychotherapy.
I. Title.   II. Polster, Richard A.
III. Series
155.4   RJ505.B4

ISBN 0-08-030985-2 (Hardcover)
ISBN 0-08-030984-4 (Flexicover)

Reproduced, printed and bound in Great Britain by Hazell Watson & Viney Limited Member of BPCC plc Aylesbury Bucks

Dedication

To Bonnie and Blaine
                  RFD

To Jodie
        RAP

Contents

PREFACE		ix
ACKNOWLEDGEMENTS		xii
1.	GETTING STARTED	1
	Overview of Teaching Methods and Principles	2
	Causes and Treatment of Childhood Disorders	4
	Skills Taught to Parents	8
	Enlisting Clients	8
	Assessing Parents	10
	The Initial Interview	11
	Facing the Challenge	21
2.	UNDERSTANDING CHILD MANAGEMENT SKILLS	23
	Skills to Increase Appropriate Behavior	23
	Skills to Decrease Inappropriate Behavior	39
3.	PUTTING IT ALL TOGETHER	56
	Compliance	56
	Child-Management Problems	65
4.	LEADING A GROUP	78
	Getting Ready	78
	Structure of Group Meetings	82
	Your Behavior	89
	One Step at a Time	90

5.	SOLVING SERVICE-DELIVERY PROBLEMS	91
	The Program Is Not Working	91
	Dropouts	102
	Hard-to-Reach Parents	104
6.	EVALUATING YOUR EFFECTIVENESS	106
	Evaluation Methods	109
	Types of Measures	110
	Experimental Designs	118
	Evaluation as an Ongoing Process	122

Afterword	124
Appendix A: Practice Records	125
Appendix B: Key points	133
Appendix C: Mastery Check Forms	141
References	149
Author Index	153
Subject Index	155
About the Authors	157
Psychology Practitioner Guidebooks List	159

Preface

Audience

This book is designed primarily for clinical practitioners who work with parents of 3- to 12-year-olds with behavior problems. If you are a social worker, school counselor, psychiatric nurse, psychologist, psychiatrist, or a family therapist, you should find the volume helpful. The particular discipline you identify with is not important. What is important is that you are faced with the challenge of helping parents to help their children. If you are a residential-care worker you may also find many of the procedures we describe useful in your work. In many ways you function as a surrogate parent. You are responsible for teaching the children in your care not only household tasks, such as making a bed and keeping a room clean, but also social skills, such as interacting with peers and making good decisions. Finally, you may find this volume useful if you are a graduate student in a helping profession. Many of you currently see families while you complete your training, or you will see families when you finish your graduate work and start your professional careers.

Development

This book represents a summary of our work with nearly 3000 families over the last 15 years. Our videotaped parenting program *WINNING!* is used in 34 states and 3 countries, and it serves as the foundation for much of the material in this guidebook. The methods we describe have been field-tested by us, as well as by dozens of other researchers and practitioners, with families from a wide variety of ethnic and socioeconomic backgrounds, and with an equally wide array of family make-ups and child behavior problems. If you are interested in our research, we refer you to R. F. Dangel and R. A. Polster (Eds.; 1984), *Parent Training: Foundations of Research and Practice.* New York: Guilford. Our methods have worked exceptionally well with many of these families, moderately well with others, and, regrettably, with some not at all. We encourage you to use the methods, to modify them, and perhaps most importantly, to evaluate them in your everyday practice. Only through this cycle will methods be sufficiently developed and refined to be of assistance to all families in need.

How This Book is Organized

This book is divided into six chapters. Chapter 1: Getting Started presents information relevant to forming parent groups, recruiting and screening parents, conducting initial interviews, forming working relationships, and completing parent-child assessments. Chapter 2: Understanding Child Management Skills, describes specific content of a group of basic child management skills. The skills are grouped according to their function: to increase behavior or to decrease behavior. Chapter 3: Putting It All Together describes how to encourage child compliance through parental requests, and how to apply the basic skills to common child management problems. This is the content you must communicate to parents if they are to understand, master, and employ each skill to its greatest advantage. Chapter 4: Leading a Group presents the steps to follow in order to equip parents with the skills you are teaching, as well as providing a weekly agenda for each of eight group meetings. Chapter 5: Solving Service-Delivery Problems describes common service-delivery problems and suggests solutions. Finally, Chapter 6: Evaluating Your Effectiveness shows how to assess the extent of change you've helped your parents achieve.

How To Use This Book

This book is designed as a guidebook. To get the best results, we recommend that you first read the entire book. Jot down your questions. Write your comments in the margin. Remember, you will be using this book — you may find yourself referring to it during a parent meeting — not just reading it and storing it on your bookshelf. When you've finished, go back and reread any sections where you have had questions. Now that you have read the entire volume, try to answer your questions. We urge you to read the entire book before you start a group, because you may find information in later chapters that could influence your treatment strategy. Once you become thoroughly familiar with the book's contents, it is time for you to start your parent group. Follow the procedures outlined in the book closely, the first few times around; as you gain experience you can modify them to fit your particular style and the needs of your parents.

We also recommend that you keep a practice log of your experiences with each family. The practice log might include comments related to methods you tried that you have found unsuccessful or successful, questions that parents ask you during a group as well as your answers, and frustrating or rewarding experiences you have with particular families. What you'll find after keeping a practice log over several groups is that you recognize those families with which you are most effective and those families for which perhaps consultation with your colleagues would be appropriate. In addition, a good practice log serves as a record of your professional development as a skilled parent trainer.

Acknowledgements

First and foremost we must thank Jerry Frank at Pergamon for his never-ending patience with us and for his understanding of academics who overcommit themselves. Dr. Paul Glasser, Dean of the Graduate School of Social Work at The University of Texas at Arlington, continues to provide an environment conducive to productivity; for this we are most grateful. To our graduate students who spent an unreasonable number of hours collecting data for us, we express our appreciation. Finally, to our professional colleagues and to the hundreds of parents from whom we've learned so very much, we simply say, "Thank you."

Chapter 1
Getting Started

Target Parents

We cannot say with any certainty for which "types" of parents our methods work best, or don't work at all. We've had many surprises. We led one of our early groups in a predominantly black inner-city housing project. Several of the mothers involved had been reported for suspected child abuse or neglect, although all were voluntary participants in our program. Although much of the available parenting literature suggested that these parents would be unresponsive and likely to discontinue participation prematurely, all but one of our initial group of 11 finished the program and all demonstrated mastery of each of the eight skills we were teaching. On the other hand, we led a group with predominantly white, educated mothers from two-parent families and found far greater reluctance to become fully involved in the program.

Some parents, who seem enthusiastic, quit; others, who seem bored, thrive. We've used our methods with two-parent and single-parent families; mothers and fathers; whites, blacks, Asians, Hispanics, and American Indians; low-income to wealthy; and PhDs to elementary school dropouts. We've served parents with 10 children or 1 child; parents whose children just recently started having difficulties and those with eight-year histories. Many, many families with each of these characteristics have benefited from the program. Unfortunately some, also with each of these characteristics, have not. We cannot identify reliably those parents most likely to be success stories, and we would argue that expensive efforts to do so divert limited resources that could be more wisely spent developing and evaluating more powerful, generalizable and predictably effective treatment strategies. Consequently, we recommend involving any parent who meets the minimal screening criteria outlined later in this chapter.

Throughout the text we make reference to "parent group" largely because we originally developed our methods for use in a group format. Given the huge numbers of families seeking assistance and the limited number of competent professionals to provide the assistance, a group format reaches more parents in less time. We and many others, however, have used very similar methods with individual parents. You should use the format that best conforms to your needs and to the needs of the population you serve.

Compatibility With Other Treatments

Families often require other services in addition to parent training. For example, you may find a multiproblem family in need of treatment for alcoholism, marriage counseling, financial planning, and housing assistance. Or you may see a parent so severely depressed that intensive individual treatment becomes critical. With cases like these, the additional services need not be incompatible with your efforts to improve the quality of the parent-child relationship. In fact, we have often found that parent training, when provided with treatment for other problems, actually improves the overall outcomes for the family. Research indicates, for example, that a depressed parent may not respond well to parent training: gains made during training may diminish quickly (Forehand & McMahon, 1981). In a case like this, we would see that the parent received treatment for depression concurrently with parent training. In this way, the treatment would help with the depression and improve the parent training as well. Some of our families have had their children temporarily removed from the home because of reports of child abuse. With these families, we involve the parents in anger-control treatment groups, marriage counseling, and relaxation training, simultaneously with parent training. In an exciting Illinois program, Project 12-Ways, John Lutzker (1984) involves his families in as many as 12 different treatments, often sequentially with parent training. You will find that virtually any other service may be provided with parent training. Of course, if multiple treatments are provided by different practitioners, close communication between everyone involved is essential to avoid conflicting treatment priorities or directions. This collaboration will enhance everyones' efforts.

OVERVIEW OF TEACHING
METHODS AND PRINCIPLES

The teaching methods we describe are based on several important principles: success, successive approximations, sequencing, multiple examples, practice, feedback, mastery, and review. You will see these emphasized throughout each chapter in the guidebook, with particular attention given to them in Chapter 4: Leading a Group. To familiarize you with them now, though, a brief description is provided here.

Getting Started

Success ranks as the most important principle to keep in mind when working with parents. Many of our parents experience constant failure, failure at work, at home, with their neighbors, their spouses, and their children. They have tried many different methods with their children: these methods too have failed. Unless they experience success with us, they will discontinue treatment. With success, they will continue to meet with us, feel good about their participation, and master new skills.

The second principle we follow is successive approximations. We don't expect our parents to learn each new skill the first time we explain or demonstrate it to them. Their first attempts will not be perfect. By focusing on the correct components of their attempts, their successive approximations, we encourage them to keep trying. We express our enthusiasm and support for any attempts they make to use the new skill. Even if their attempts are fumbling, incorrect, or only remotely related to what we are teaching, they are nonetheless approximations. Over time, with our feedback, these successive approximations gradually look more and more like the skill we are after.

We also emphasize sequencing by both difficulty and by prerequisite analyses in our attempts to teach child management skills. Since we want our parents to experience success, we begin with easy skills first, then progress to the more difficult ones. This increases our parents' chances for success. Regardless of the skill we're teaching, we only teach it after parents have mastered prerequisite skills. For example, when we teach descriptive praise, which sounds something like, "Hello Johnny, you sure did a nice job hanging up your clothes today," we first make sure the parents know how to describe what they see. If we attempt to teach skills that are not sequenced both by difficulty and prerequisite analyses, our parents suffer the consequence: they fail.

The use of multiple examples provides us with another guiding principle. The most effective way to communicate to a parent what we want them to do is to give many, many examples. The more examples we provide, and the more diverse the examples, the greater our chances that our parents will master the skill. We have found that we just cannot provide too many examples. In a lengthy series of several examples, there may be only one that hits home for a particular parent. In the absence of meaningful examples, the parents don't recognize the applicability of the skill to their situation and they may not learn it.

Practice also represents an important principle we emphasize throughout this book. Whenever we teach a new skill to a parent, practice constitutes a majority of our work. The more we can encourage parents to practice the skill, under many diverse circumstances and with their own children, the more progress we see. We incorporate practice into each group session.

Feedback plays a significant part in our teaching of child management skills. With feedback parents learn exactly how to execute each new skill. We provide clear, precise feedback, and we make certain that most of our feedback is positive. As a rule, for every one bit of corrective feedback, we provide at least four bits that focus on some good quality of the performance. We have found that most parents respond well to feedback given within these parameters.

Another important method we recommend is mastery criteria. We find the best way to insure that parents learn the skills we are teaching is by requiring some objective mastery criteria: a concrete way to see that the parents can demonstrate the skill. Typically, mastery criteria are stated in terms of how often and under what conditions the parents must use the skill. For example, when we teach descriptive praise, we set a mastery criteria of five descriptive praises in a 5-minute period. We have found that in the absence of specific mastery criteria, parents do not learn the skills well enough to leave the training situation, return home, and use the skills correctly with their children.

The final characteristic we consider to be very important is review. We start each session by reviewing the material that we have covered in prior sessions. This review helps parents remember previously introduced concepts, keeps them from getting rusty in their use of past skills, and underscores the importance of continued use of each skill. Review also can point out those skill and content areas that require additional instruction.

Our methods are not intended to be used for crisis intervention. Families in crisis require immediate service and release from overwhelming stress. When families under these circumstances seek our assistance, we either provide short-term crisis intervention or we refer them to an appropriate resource in the community. Once the crisis has been resolved, we follow-up to then offer parent training. Trying to involve parents in systematic, skill-oriented parent training when they are in crisis results in failure and dissatisfaction and must be considered unethical.

CAUSES AND TREATMENT OF CHILDHOOD DISORDERS

Assumptions

Our parenting work rests on three major assumptions. The first assumption is that all behavior is learned. This includes not only the nice behaviors that children do, such as saying please, thank you, cleaning up their rooms, sharing, showing curiosity, and laughing, but also the not-so-nice behaviors such as temper tantrums, fighting, crying, backtalking, whining, and refusing to do as asked. All behavior develops in the same way, as a result of an interaction between the child and things that occur in the child's environment.

The second assumption is that parents can have control of those things in the environment that contribute to the current behavior of the child. Although the parents may not recognize that they have this control, or they may not use the control in order to produce the results they prefer, they nonetheless can have the control. Our job is to help them use their control to promote healthy child development and improved parent-child relationships.

Our third assumption is that the precise causes of a particular childhood behavior problem may be indeterminable. Sure, with regard to any individual case, we can speculate that perhaps the problem originated because of this reason or that, but this is, in fact, just speculation. It is very difficult, perhaps impossible, to identify retrospectively with any certainty that a particular behavior occurred as a result of some particular event. Furthermore it is not necessary to determine what caused a particular behavior: the fact of the matter is that the behavior exists. The task at hand is to assist the parents in learning more effective ways to deal with the problem.

Changing Behavior is Difficult

The most difficult task you face will be teaching parents to change their behavior. When you and your parents embark on a behavior-change program, remember that you combat the history of both the parent and the child. The parent has behaved in a certain way with her child, using certain skills for quite some time. Furthermore, she has listened to advice from friends, family, clergy, Ann Landers, Dear Abby, Phil Donahue, Dr. Spock, Jim and Tammy Bakker, and Roseann Roseannadanna. She has tried countless methods to influence her child. All of these unsuccessful attempts both contribute to her learning history and work against your success. Furthermore, when a parent changes her behavior, she combats her child's history. Her child has behaved in a certain way for quite some time. Now his mama behaves differently and expects him to behave differently. But remember, because the child has behaved in a certain way for quite some time, his behavior may not be any more maleable than mom's. Many instances must occur before the child recognizes and responds to the new rules. One way to conceptualize this problem is to imagine a scale. In the middle of this scale is a fulcrum. The left side of the scale, which is weighted quite heavily, represents mom's current parenting style. The right side of the scale, which is empty, represents the methods you are teaching. The left side clearly weighs more than the right side and, to carry the analogy further, is much more likely to occur. Each trial and each experience that the parent has using the methods you teach tips the scale to the right. One experience contributes just a tiny little bit to the weight on the right side of the scale. But each attempt does tilt the balance a little more in your favor. Your job is to encourage the parent to practice the skills with sufficient frequency so that the scale eventually tips to the right. The more likely response from mom then becomes the one you've taught.

Meeting Parent Resistance

Parents often resist involvement in parent training. They may express reservations such as, "The program sounds really worthwhile. I hope I can make the meetings on Tuesday. I'm kinda busy right now," or "The last parent group I was in never really got off the ground. Most of the people stopped coming after about the third session." Sometimes their resistance takes a different form: they don't show up for appointments, they don't implement agreed-upon treatment strategies, they misplace data-collection sheets, they send the kids to spend the week with long-lost relatives, or they report instant and miraculous improvement in their children's behavior. Although it's difficult to determine why resistance occurs, three methods will help decrease client resistance. First, we recommend that you bring the issue out in the open with the parent.

> Mrs. Mason: Yes, I can probably attend meetings on Tuesday mornings unless something else comes up. Sometimes K-Marts has big Blue Light Specials on Tuesdays and you know how tight my budget is. I can't afford to miss those sales!
> Counselor: Yes, Mrs. Mason, I do know how careful you are with your money. It will be really important for you to attend every meeting though – if we are to make progress with Marsha. I'll need for you to understand the group has to come before anything else for the next eight Tuesday mornings. Can you make this kind of agreement and really live up to it?
> Counselor: So, Mr. Carrill, you and your wife have tried praising Tyler before and that didn't seem to make any difference, is that right?
> Mr. Carrill: That's right. The last counselor we saw insisted that if we just praised, praised, praised Tyler – everything would work out just fine. But it didn't. Now it sounds like you're going to tell us to do the same thing.
> Counselor: I appreciate your sharing with me your concerns about what we're covering here. That really helps me know where you're coming from and gives me some ideas about what we need to focus on. I'm sure you'll find some major differences between the methods we'll focus on in this group compared with what you've learned elsewhere.
> Mrs. Landers: I forgot to bring back that sheet you asked me to fill out. I started to do it but then decided that I'd just tell you because it seemed to be more less a waste of time. There was nothing on there you didn't already know.
> Counselor: Ann, I'm glad the information we agreed to collect seems to be turning out to look like we guessed it would. I'm concerned, though, that this is the third week now that you've forgotten to bring the homework. Let's talk about that. Sometimes when parents keep forgetting their homework it indicates they've lost interest in the program or they have some doubts about whether the program is any good for them. How do you feel now about this?

Are there some things maybe we should discuss? I really want this to help you and Abby, and the only way this will happen is if we are very honest and frank with each other.

Counselor: (On telephone) Hello, Mrs. Donohue, this is Ms. Griffen calling. How are you today? I'm calling to confirm our next parent group meeting on Wednesday afternoon at 3:00.

Mrs. Donohue: I don't think I'll be able to make it. Sarah has her club meeting then.

Counselor: I'm real sorry to hear that you won't be able to make the meeting, Mrs. Donohue, especially since you missed last week too. It's going to be very difficult for us to catch up.

Mrs. Donohue: Well, I will try to come.

Counselor: Mrs. Donohue, we are starting to make some progress with Sarah and I hope we can continue. How do you think she is doing? Are there some things happening we need to check out? I'd sure hate to lose you from the group.

The second method you can try in order to reduce resistance is to make certain the parent understands what it is you're introducing. If the parent does not understand an assignment, she will be less likely to comply and you may misinterpret her behavior as a lack of motivation.

Counselor: Mr. Wright, how did Deirdra respond when you tried using "time-out" last week?

Parent: I did't get around to using it because everything was great last week. Deirdra did everything I asked her to do.

Counselor: You mentioned you had an episode where she was beating on her little brother. That's just like in the examples we talked about last week. Do you think time-out would have been something to try then? How could it have been used?

Parent: I'm not really sure, since you said not to send her to her room.

Counselor: Well, Mr. Wright, you're right. Sending Deirdra to her room probably wouldn't work too well, because she has a TV, telephone, and stereo in it. Some other places that can be used for time-out include a corner in the kitchen, or the chair in the den, as long as no TV, books, or conversation is available.

Parent: Oh, I see. I didn't realize I could use any of those. I'll give it a try next time and see what happens.

Counselor: Terrific! We'll be looking forward to hearing the results.

Finally, make sure the parent clearly understands the benefits to be gained by participating in the program. Be as specific and concrete as you can. It's much more useful for a parent to know exactly what to expect than to proceed with just some vague idea about what might happen.

Counselor: Mrs. Tanner, I've noticed some reluctance on your part to stick with the program. You've missed the last two sessions and your homework hasn't been completed. I know you're very, very busy with 7 other children and working full time. It is next to impossible to take on any additional activities. But I also know what a terribly rough time Demetrius has been giving you and how upset you've been over the whole thing.

Parent: Yes, Demetrius is still getting into trouble. My next door neighbor told me yesterday she was no longer letting her children play with him anymore because she considers him a bad influence. And, the school called wanting to give him a spanking — the third one in three days. This time for spitting in the principal's face.

Counselor: Wow! You're getting it from every direction. Look, these are problems that we can help you with in the group. You'll learn how to handle his fighting with other kids in the neighborhood and his vulgar language. You'll also see how to increase his cooperation with the teachers at school. But it's going to take a lot of work from you and from all of us in the group to solve these problems. I'm just afraid if we don't do this now, the problems with Demetrius will continue — maybe even get worse.

SKILLS TAUGHT TO PARENTS

We have selected only decidedly behavioral parenting skills for inclusion in this text. Strong empirical support for the skills exists in the child development and behavioral psychology literature (see for example Gordon & Davidson, 1981). Parents receive the skills well and find them helpful. Of course, countless other skills useful to parents exist, and for use with a particular family you may want to identify specific skills not included here. You can use the same methods we describe in Chapter 4 to teach additional skills you consider important.

The parenting skills we focus on are grouped into three main categories: The first category includes skills designed primarily to increase appropriate child behavior: praise, rewards and privileges, and suggestive praise. The second category includes skills to decrease inappropriate behavior: ignoring or extinction, removing rewards and privileges, time-out, and spanking. The third group of skills covered in the text focuses on combining these methods to increase child compliance with parent requests and to solve specific child management problems.

ENLISTING CLIENTS

If you work at an agency with an existing pool of parents who request parent-training services, you are set to begin client assessment and screening. However, many of you must enlist clients from other agencies. For example, if you are a psychologist or social worker at a mental health center, you may work with a state department of child protective services. In situations like these, one of your first tasks will be to let agencies within your community know that you are offering parent-education services. All agencies that serve parents or children should be notified, because they may have parents in need of the service and may become active referral sources. We have received referrals from the public schools, local child-abuse units, mental health centers, hospitals, residential treatment facilities, day-care centers, volunteer organizations, and graduates from our previous groups.

To begin developing a referral network, you will need a package of information to distribute to agencies. Potential referring agencies generally prefer something written that they can reread at a later date. Include in the package a statement of the purpose of your parenting group, a description of the appropriate parents to refer to the group, a list of any fees that parents will be charged in order for them to participate, and instructions on how the agency refers a parent to you.

Practitioners who are asked to refer parents must understand exactly what they can expect their clients to receive. Fortunately, practitioners protect their clients and are reluctant to make referrals unless they are confident that their clients will receive quality services.

Schedule an appointment with agency staff to discuss the service you aim to provide. Simply distributing materials through the mail, without the face-to-face contact, just does not work. Present a description of the service you offer and distribute the information packages you have developed. This helps the agency staff know exactly what your services are about and it makes it easier for them to decide which of their clients might benefit from participation. Be honest and forthright. Experienced practitioners know that no single service provides all the answers for a given family; every service has both its strong points and its weak. On occasion we have found it productive to make our presentation to several key staff over lunch, at our expense. The relaxed atmosphere facilitates the exchange of information.

Always make the procedure as easy as possible for the referring agency. For example, if you ask an agency to complete paperwork, keep the paperwork simple. Don't ask them for information that you can obtain yourself or that you will not be using. A follow-up visit or phone call after your presentation to staff is a must; it conveys a sincere interest in wanting to provide the service. Likewise, you may want to provide information to the referring agency about how their referrals are doing once they begin participation with you.

When you contact parents that have been referred to you, identify yourself, the agency you represent, and the referral source. This helps the parents feel at ease and lets them know that the service you are offering is legitimate. Briefly describe your program and what the parents can achieve from participation. If they express interest, schedule an initial interview at their convenience. How you present yourself during this initial telephone conversation greatly influences both whether parents decide to schedule an initial interview as well as the early stages of their relationship with you. If they find you warm, responsive, and understanding, they will be more likely to participate than if they find you abrupt, mechanical, and distant.

The most reliable way to develop a referral network is to provide quality service to parents. Once you have led several parent groups and helped the participants, they will let other parents know. If they were referred by a practitioner in the community, the practitioner will learn that you can be counted on to provide a useful service. Subsequent referrals will follow. On the other hand, sloppy or insensitive work generates bad feelings and reluctance on the part of professionals to send their clients to you.

ASSESSING PARENTS

Appropriate Interviewer Behavior

Many of the points described here refer to your behavior during the initial interview but apply equally throughout all meetings with parents. Your behavior during the initial interview influences the amount and accuracy of the information they provide, how much rapport they feel with you and thus their willingness to cooperate with your requests, and the likelihood they will participate in the service. For these reasons you must pay particular attention to both the information you present and the way you present it. There is no substitute for showing warmth, empathy, and sensitivity to the stress faced by the parents. Not only are they pressured by the problems with their children, but they may also have apprehensions about seeking help. Worse, they may have sought help previously and been unsuccessful.

Matching the parents' language will help put them at ease and increase their confidence in you. This doesn't mean you must be phony or insincere; it means that you must be sensitive to individual differences in educational, cultural, ethnic, and socioeconomic backgrounds. If parents feel you are talking down to them or using 25-cent words when nickle ones would do just fine, they aren't likely to open up. On the other hand, because one of the most visible characteristics parents have with which to evaluate you is your language, if they leave feeling like you all heard each other, their evaluation of you will be higher.

Let the parents know that you don't blame them – that everyone suffers in situations like theirs. Comments like "Kids can really be tough sometimes," "It seems like we try our best and things still don't go the way we would like," and "Wow, it really gets exhausting dealing with this day after day" communicate understanding. Parents will realize you don't attribute fault to them, that you realize their intentions are the best or they wouldn't be in your office in the first place!

One of the most important points for you to make early on is that the situation can be changed. Things will get better. Convey a sense of optimism.

Let the parents know that yes, their problems can be solved, and yes, their children can be helped. Tell them about families with similar problems that have been helped. Give them something to look forward to. At the same time you'll also want to communicate clearly that this won't happen with the wave of your magic wand (no matter how well endowed you may be) without considerable work — work from you and work from the parents. Now is the time to let them know they face a challenging job. You will be there as much as necessary, but their full cooperation and commitment are essential.

By the time many parents are interested in parenting services, they feel a great deal of frustration, anger, and depression. The first step in helping to remedy this situation is simply to be a good listener. Your time will be well spent: parents will begin to trust you and to realize that you are interested in assisting them. You will also be able to use the information the parents provide you in order to complete your assessment and to make certain that you are sensitive to their concerns throughout their participation in the program.

Avoid any sign of defensiveness or "I know it all." Don't offer suggestions, don't offer remedies, don't provide answers. Chances are good that at this stage you'd be wrong! Most parents find defensiveness and premature advice-giving objectionable; this discourages parents from sharing with you information that could be helpful later and it limits your search for other relevant information.

Find things to agree with the parents about. If they describe their son as a no-good-for-nothing bum, you can reply with, "Yep, David has really been giving you a hard time. It's become a major battle just to get him ready for school in the morning." They will see your agreement as understanding and be all the more willing to accept your future suggestions. Of course, you'll want to be honest: Don't agree when you disagree. But do actively look for comments by the parents that are in accord with the direction you'll be taking in treatment. Related to this is self-disclosure. When appropriate, feel free to share with parents the situations you've been in that resemble theirs.

> Parent: My daughter just will not go to bed at night. She gets up 15 times for a drink of water, to say good night, because she doesn't feel well, because she heard a noise.
> Counselor: I know what you mean. When my son was four, I thought for a while there he was going to stay awake for the entire year.

THE INITIAL INTERVIEW

Assessing the Problem

In many ways, the initial interview is the most difficult session to conduct because you have so many tasks to complete and so much rests on your skill at accomplishing these tasks. During the initial interview you must: (a) begin to establish a working relationship, (b) assess the nature of the difficulties the parent is having, (c) describe the service you can provide, (d) engage the parent in service or make an appropriate referral, and (e) obtain a commitment to cooperate. Each of these tasks is described below.

Much of the material presented in the section Appropriate Interviewer Behavior applies here. In addition, you should start the session off with a warm greeting and the expected social amenities. Be sure to thank the parents for attending and don't miss the opportunity to reinforce them for showing such interest in their children.

> Counselor: Hello, Mr. and Mrs. Finster. Can I get you a cup of coffee or a soft drink before we get started?
> Mr. Finster: Do you have anything harder? I think we're going to need it! (Laughter)
> Counselor: No, I'm afraid not, Mr. Finster, but the coffee has a lot of caffeine in it.
> Mrs. Finster: I'll take a cup.
> Mr. Finster: Me too, thanks.
> Counselor: First off, I'd like to thank you both for coming in this afternoon. I realize you had to leave work early and get a babysitter. That kind of interest in your kids will really help us get a lot done here.

Parents are often eager to tell you about their children. Now is the time for you to begin your fact finding. This is when you start to define the problem, its nature, magnitude, and duration. You'll also want to investigate what past attempts the parents have made to solve the problem and other family circumstances that may help or impede progress.

> Counselor: Mr. Finster, why don't we go ahead and get started. Can you tell me a little about the sorts of difficulties Johnny has been having?
> Mrs. Finster: I can, since I'm the one who has to put up with his poor attitude and disrespect. He won't do a thing I say unless I threaten to beat him or tell his father. He hits his little sister, he cusses, the other kids in the neighborhood aren't allowed to play with him. You know it's pretty bad when the other mothers in the neighborhood won't let their kids play with yours. They call him a troublemaker.
> Counselor: He's really giving you a run for your money, isn't he?
> Mrs. Finster: You haven't heard the half of it. Last week I sent him to his room for kicking the dog and found out he crawled through the bedroom window and was outside playing.
> Counselor: What did you do then?
> Mrs. Finster: I told his father.
> Mr. Finster: The minute I walk through the door every night it's the same thing. Johnny did this, Johnny did that. I'm supposed to tear into him for stuff he did hours or even days earlier. He's okay with me. When I tell him to do something, he does it.

Mrs. Finster: That's not true. Lots of times you have to threaten him too. And you always have to tell him three or four times before he'll do anything. I don't know how much longer I can take this. He treats me like a piece of garbage, someone to feed him and clean his clothes and that's it. I've about had it. Plus it's putting a lot of stress on our marriage. I can't get close to Big David [Mr. Finster] when I'm fighting with Johnny, but he can't seem to understand that.

Counselor: You've just about had it, huh? What things have you all tried to get Johnny to behave better?

Mr. Finster: About two years ago he saw a counselor at school because he was getting into a lot of trouble there. it seemed to help; at least we stopped getting so many complaints from the school.

Counselor: Why did he stop going?

Mrs. Finster: We had to have him change schools because we moved.

Counselor: So, the problems with Johnny have been going on since he was in the third grade. Is that correct?

Mrs. Finster: Yes; before then everything seemed fine. He had plenty of friends, although he has always been a bully and had a smart mouth on him.

Counselor: Tell me, Mr. Finster, it doesn't sound like you're quite as convinced as your wife that Johnny has a problem. What do you think?

Mr. Finster: He can be obstinate at times, but part of it is just "boys will be boys." I would like him to not be so rough on his mother, though, and to do what we say without an argument every time.

If a parent reports that she has tried counseling before and it has been unsuccessful, ask her why it was unsuccessful and try to separate your approach from the other. Point out dissimilarities.

Counselor: Mrs. Mendes, you mentioned that you and your daughter saw a psychologist last year but it didn't seem to help. What did you do in treatment?

Mrs. Mendes: Well, it was kinda weird. He kept wanting me to tell him about my relationship with my mother and father. he also asked me to keep a diary of my dreams. I really couldn't see what my dreams had to do with Julie's temper tantrums in school.

Counselor: I'm sorry your last attempt didn't work out. It's always disappointing when you put forth so much effort to solve a problem and get nowhere. I think you'll find our approach here considerably different. We'll spend a great deal of time looking at Julie's temper tantrums and different ways to handle them – and absolutely no time talking about your dreams.

Determine if other community resources, either in addition to or in place of parent training, are necessary. You can best accomplish this by doing a brief survey of several life areas that may require attention. These areas include health, marriage, family relationships, sex, finances, religion, in-laws, and employment. Bring up any others you believe are important.

Counselor: Ms. Epson, you've given me a lot of useful information about your son, William. I think I know pretty well what sorts of things he's doing that make it so rough for you. If we may, I'd like to switch topics for a few minutes and talk about some other things. Sometimes if we have other problems or stressful situations going on in our lives they can affect how we interact with our children. For example, if I have an especially long day at work, I may not be interested in singing "Old MacDonald" with my daughter. Do you follow me?

Ms. Epson: Yes, I do. All my days are long. And now that my divorce is final it seems like I have no time to myself. It's go to work, come home, cook, clean up the dishes, put William to bed, do the laundry, straighten up the house, pay the bills, go to bed, and start over.

Counselor: You are really busy! And under pressure, too. Does it get to you?

Ms. Epson: Yeah. Most of the time I feel down in the dumps. To put it another way, I have to look up to see bottom. The other day I parachuted off the thin side of a dime, and if I were any lower I'd be in China.

Counselor: Ms. Epson, I think maybe we should spend some time seeing what we can do to help you start to feel better about your situation. I don't know how long a person can stand so much pressure.

Ms. Epson: (tears in her eyes) I think it's hopeless. Sometimes I even think I should send William to a computer camp and end it all.

In this example, the counselor has recognized that Ms. Epson is severely depressed and will require individual counseling in addition to participating in the parenting program. The counselor assists her in making an appointment with a staff member at his agency.

Before you begin to describe in more detail the service you are providing, you should have a clear understanding of the difficulties the parent is having with her child, as well as any other problems that may require treatment or referral. To assist you in completing this stage of assessment, in addition to the clinical interview, you may find it helpful to use other assessment methods.

Pencil-and-paper checklists. Pencil-and-paper checklists and scales sometimes produce a great deal of useful information very quickly and inexpensively. The Parent Attitudes Test (PAT) (Cowen, Huser, Beach, & Rappaport, 1970) measures several dimensions of parent attitudes toward the child's behavior and adjustment at home and school. The Becker Bipolar Adjective Checklist (Becker, 1960) is also a convenient tool to gather a comprehensive overview of the extent of child problems identified by the parent. A variety of other pencil-and-paper checklists are widely used as well. Select those that best collect the type of information you'll actually be using, that are convenient to administer and score, that can be easily read and understood by your parent population, and that attempt to measure actual behavior rather than "traits" or internal personality characteristics that may appear to be less amenable to change.

Direct observation. Direct observation in the home may illustrate many parent-child interactional patterns better than does any other assessment method. Direct observation is expensive and time consuming, but the results often outweigh these considerations. Many times we have found that parent descriptions don't match what occurs. Parents may be too upset with the situation or too involved in past incidents to describe accurately what happens today. For example, we worked with one mother whose husband had recently reenlisted in the army for a second 4-year term overseas without first discussing it with her. She described her son, who happened to be a dead ringer for his father, as refusing to do anything she asked, a bed-wetter, with no friends in the neighborhood and in frequent trouble at school. Our direct observations revealed quite the contrary: The child had many friends, did virtually everything his mother requested, was on the honor roll at school, and was terribly embarrassed at even the mention of enuresis. Clearly, mom's distorted perceptions, not her son's "deviant" behavior, required attention. In other families, although they may not be so extreme, parent reports sometimes overestimate or underestimate the magnitude, duration, or frequency of a problem. Direct observation can provide a reliability check on their reports.

To collect observational data for clinical purposes (rather than for scientific evaluation) we recommend the use of simple frequency data. Frequency data is easy to collect, is accurate, is suitable for behaviors that typically have a clear beginning and end, and provides a great deal of information. To collect frequency data, you first need to develop specific definitions for those behaviors of interest. Usually an hour of observational data collected three times before you begin treatment is sufficent for you to get a picture of what is going on. Collect the data at times that are recommended by the parent: Make sure the parent, child, and perhaps siblings will be present, that distractions such as visitors will be minimized and, if possible, select times when the problems of concern are likely to occur (for example, at bedtime, while getting ready for school in the morning, or just before dinner).

While you collect observational data, a few simple rules will help to keep the data accurate and objective. First, don't discuss anything with the parents during data collection. Ask them to pretend you are invisible. Second, don't share with them the data you collect until treatment begins; otherwise they may react and artificially distort the information you get. Finally, once you start actual data collection, stick to your definitions. Don't keep changing the definitions to fit what you see; otherwise any change between the data you collect before treatment and the data you collect during and after treatment may be due to a gradual shifting in your interpretation of the definitions.

Parent self-report. A third assessment method frequently used is parent self-report. Parent self-report involves asking the parent to collect information systematically about some particular event. For example, you may want Mrs. Shannon to determine how often her daughter, Patti, wets her pants, or you may want Mr. Kersey to ascertain exactly when Jose uses foul language. To employ parent self-report, make sure the instructions you give to the parent are specific and clear. The more precise the assignment, the greater the likelihood that the parent will comply. To use our two examples, instead of saying to Mrs. Shannon, "Pay attention to how often Patti wets her pants," say "Mrs. Shannon, I'm drawing up a form here for us to use to keep track of how often Patti wets her pants. I'd like you to post the form on the refrigerator door so you'll see it often and remember to use it. Each day check every time Patti wets her pants so much that she has to change them. Do you understand?" Drawing up a form and filling in a sample of the information you want is also helpful. We always make a duplicate copy for the parent's file in case the parent misplaces the original.

In addition to making sure your assignments are specific and clear, you should also give the parent rationales about why you are asking her to collect the information. Some sample rationales include: Collecting information about how Sally behaves on a day-to-day basis lets us know how serious a problem we are dealing with; your reports keep us informed about our progress; or what we are really interested in is changes Debbie makes on a day-to-day basis at home and school. The information you collect tells us this; and, if we don't see the kind of improvements we want in the information you collect, we know we need to take a look at our methods to see what needs to be changed!

If parents understand why they are collecting information and how important it is, they will become more actively involved as a partner in the treatment process. You must reinforce parents for collecting data when they do. If they bring in their completed self-report form and you ignore it, they will learn quickly that the assignment isn't important and that they aren't truly involved. Both of these outcomes are tremendously detrimental. If you've asked a parent to collect some information, *begin* the next session with a review of what she's done. A phone call or two between sessions can work wonders to stress the importance of parent self-report data. You'll find that if you call the first couple of times you give an assignment, parent compliance will be high and you won't need to call after about the second or third week.

Child interviews. We often find it helpful to interview the child as part of our assessment, especially if the child is at least 5 years old. Children have a remarkable ability to describe what's going on at home from a perspective sometimes radically different from that of their parents. You may find, for example, that Cinderella has only started to refuse to do her chores since her stepsisters moved in, something her parents forgot to mention during their interview with you. On the other hand, the child may provide corroboration for exactly what the parents have explained. Either outcome gives you information useful for you to complete a thorough and accurate assessment.

Existing records. Existing records and collateral reports from others may also help to complete the picture, and they can save you time and the parents the agony of repeating the same story for the fifteenth time. Of course, you'll want to verify the accuracy of the information contained in existing records and if you contact others, such as schoolteachers, relatives, clergy, or past counselors, you'll need written permission from the parent. If the child is at least 8 years old we recommend discussing the matter with the child as well.

Describing the Service

The second major task to complete during the initial interview is to describe the service you are providing. This gives the parents a chance to determine if they see a match between their needs and your service, and it gives you the chance to begin the role-induction process. You should describe the purpose of the service, the format you'll follow, what benefits the parents can reasonably expect to gain from participation, and what responsibilities and obligations you and the parents each have.

The purpose of the parent group is to help parents learn specific skills they can use to improve their relationships with their children and to solve common child management problems they may be having. The group is not a traditional therapy group in that the primary focus is on the acquisition of skills related to a narrowly defined area rather than on gaining insight or making major personality or character changes. Many parents find this purpose to be less threatening; they aren't "sick" or "in therapy" — they are learning new skills.

The format is small group, usually involving 8 to 10 parents, mothers and fathers. Meetings are held once per week and last $1\frac{1}{2}$ hours. The basic group continues for 8 weeks, with advanced meetings held as needed and after completion of the basic group. During a group meeting, parents will exchange information about their children and the difficulties they are having. All information is strictly confidential. Each week, the group leader will present information about a new skill. The information will include a description of the skill and under what conditions and for what problems the skill is appropriate. The leader will demonstrate the skill and provide many examples of its use. Parents will then have the opportunity to practice the skill during the group and will receive constructive feedback about its use. A simple homework assignment will be given each week, wherein parents will be asked to practice a skill with their children.

By participation in the group, parents can expect to gain improved relationships with their children. They should become more effective teachers as well. In addition, they should feel more confident in their abilities to solve any new problems that may arise. Their children's appropriate behavior should increase and they should be happier.

To realize these gains, parents must participate fully in each group meeting. They must attempt to learn each new skill and to understand how and when it should be used. They must report accurately what happens when they practice the skill at home with their children, and they must complete each weekly homework assignment. They should also discuss any problems they may have with mastering each skill as well as any philosophical objections they may harbor.

As the group leader, you must present the relevant information in a way that is understood by the parents; assist them in completing the homework assignments; and provide detailed and accurate feedback about their skill acquisition during the group practice exercises. Your feedback should be presented in a way that is nonthreatening and that emphasizes the positive. You should respect their rights as parents and try to understand any philosophical objections they may have to anything you are teaching. You should also appreciate that no one has all the answers.

Engaging the Parent in Treatment

Several factors influence which families will benefit most from the services you are offering. Before you solidify the parents' involvement in your service you should do some preliminary screening to make sure the parents are likely to benefit from service. Because the methods we describe in this book are designed primarily for parents of 3-year-olds to 12-year-olds, first make certain that the children fall within the proper age range. Occasionally we work with a parent whose child is 13 or 14 or 1 or 2, depending on the capabilities of the child and the problems of concern to the parent. However, if a parent comes looking for help with an acting-out teenager, we make a referral.

Secondly, make certain the parent has access to the children. Many times parents whom we work with have children in temporary foster placement because of suspected child abuse. Or the parents are divorced and the parent requesting service does not have regular visitation with the children. Since our teaching methods focus heavily on practice and actual interaction with the children, parents must have access to the children. If this requirement cannot be met, the service will be of little benefit and a referral is probably wise. We have been successful working with state child-protective-service agencies to arrange for children in custody to be returned home for several hours each week, under supervision, to permit the parent the opportunity to participate in the service and to learn new parenting skills.

Another point to consider is whether the person you are interviewing is the primary caretaker. From time to time, a grandmother will contact us to express concern over the way her daughter is raising a child and to enroll in our service. We appreciate grandma's interest, but because she is not the primary caretaker, and is not in a position to influence the primary caretaker, we have found generally that parent training is not the appropriate service in such instances. Likewise, we sometimes see a mom who requests service, only to discover that mom works afternoons and weekends and primary child-care responsibility rests with an older sibling. Again, we might enlist the sibling, provide other services to the mom, or make a referral.

When you've determined that the children are the right age, that the parent has access to the children, and that the person requesting the service is the primary caretaker, you are then ready to examine your assessment data to determine whether your service is the one best suited to meeting the needs of the parent and child. Your service teaches child management skills. If a parent comes to you with a problem not related to child management, for example a custody battle, or with a problem you consider yourself unfamiliar with, uninterested in, or incapable of handling, discuss the case with a colleague or make a referral.

Another important dimension to consider is whether prerequisite services are required. Again, the empirical literature suggests that such family problems as pending divorce, serious parental depression, insularity, and alcoholism require concurrent or prerequisite services to enhance parent-training effectiveness. If these or other problems that might interfere with the success of the parent training exist, we encourage the parent to seek services and we assist in arranging them.

The final issue we address is parent interest. If during the initial interview the parent expresses concern, reluctance, or lack of interest, we discuss these then rather than after the parent starts the program. We have found that by dealing with any reservations up front, the parents are more likely to feel committed to the program and to participate fully. On the other hand, if we ignore this feedback from the parents and fail to address their concerns, we risk not gaining their full cooperation and losing them before they benefit from the service. You should encourage parents to discuss any concerns openly, and you should provide them with honest, forthright, and accurate answers. Any misrepresentation or misunderstanding introduced at this time will come back to haunt you later. Even if they disagree with your position, they will appreciate your openness. If you or the parents feel these concerns cannot be adequately addressed and there are still reservations about participating in the service, invite the parents to consider alternative services.

To summarize, you should investigate several areas as part of the task of engaging parents in your service. You'll want to make certain the children of concern are between the ages of 3 and 12; that the parent who requests service has regular access to the children and is the primary caretaker; that the service you're offering is appropriate for the problems of concern to the parent; that any essential prerequisite services are available; and finally, that parents fully understand their and your responsibilities and are interested in participating. Once you've checked out these areas, you are ready to close the initial interview by obtaining a commitment to cooperate and by scheduling the next meeting.

Commitment to Cooperate

A commitment to cooperate is a verbal or written statement from the parent, agreeing to participate fully in the service you are providing. Before you obtain a commitment to cooperate, you should reiterate for the parent exactly what is expected of those participating in the service. You'll want to summarize what participation involves: attending a minimum of eight group meetings; participating in role-play exercises during the meetings; completing homework practice assignments; and discussing with other parents both successful and unsuccessful attempts at learning new skills. Once this is clear, ask if the parent is willing to participate. This verbal commitment will help to facilitate participation and attendance throughout the course of treatment. This step in the initial interview might sound like the one below.

>   Counselor: Well, Mr. Mindel. I think we've gotten a lot done this morning. You've given me a very clear understanding of the difficulties you're having with Elizabeth and Allison, and I'm convinced that we can be of assistance to you in solving these problems.
>   Mr. Mindel: That's good to hear, although I'm not completely convinced. I've had trouble with my kids since they was born and their mother, Gloria, ran away with Welch.
>   Counselor: For sure you're right about one thing, Mr. Mindel. We have our work cut out for us. We aren't going to change things over night and we're all going to have to give it our best shot. But if we do, I think we can see some positive results.
>   Mr. Mindel: When does the program start?
>   Counselor: The next group starts in just about two weeks. To participate, you'll have to attend the eight group meetings we talked about, and during the group meetings we'll be practicing some new ways to deal with our children.

We'll also have homework assignments to practice things every week between meetings. Sometimes what we try will work great – other times not so great. Either way we'll be talking in the group with the other parents about how things went.

Mr. Mindel: Okay.

Counselor: Mr. Mindel, do you have any questions about anything we've discussed? I want to make certain that you understand what it is we'll be doing in the group and what is expected of you.

Mr. Mindel: I think I understand. What happens if I have to miss a meeting though? Sometimes I have to work overtime.

Counselor: We're all extra busy these days. Seems like there is never enough time to get everything done we have to do. Each meeting will bring up a real specific method to try with our kids, so if you miss a meeting, you'll miss everything we cover that week. It will be very important for you to try to make it every time.

Mr. Mindel: I'll try, for sure. But if the boss says "Work a double shift tonight," I need the money and I can't turn him down or it goes on my record.

Counselor: If you absolutely have to miss, call ahead of time, the minute you find out you won't be able to make it. That way we can tell the other members of the group not to expect you. We will be spending some time each meeting reviewing what we've covered the week before, so that will help. And I will be willing to meet with you individually after the group to help you catch up. Course, the best thing to do is to make each meeting. Eight weeks will go pretty fast and you'll be happy with the results you see, too – if you stick with it.

Mr. Mindel: Let's see, you said the meetings are Monday nights at 6:30, right?

Counselor: Yep. Now that you understand what we'll be doing and what's expected of you, Mr. Mindel, are you willing to participate?

Mr. Mindel: I sure want to give it a try. Something's got to be done about my girls before they end up in a home for unwed mothers or a juvenile delinquency farm.

Counselor: We'll be able to make some progress if we work hard and participate each week. And it sure sounds like you're interested in doing the best you can for your girls. I'll see you then on Monday evening at 6:30, two weeks from yesterday, on March 30. Here is an appointment card. Be sure to call if anything comes up. See you then, Mr. Mindel.

FACING THE CHALLENGE

Getting ready to lead a successful parent group requires a great deal of work on your part. The more organized and thorough you are in your early preparation, the greater the benefits your participants will receive. Educating community agencies that you provide parenting services will facilitate your development of a referral network and help you to reach those families in need. Providing quality services will insure your success and the success of the parents you aim to assist.

The initial interview demands considerable skill: you must assess the presenting problems, describe the service you provide, determine if a good fit exists between your service and the needs of the parent, engage the parent in treatment, obtain a commitment to cooperate, and schedule the first meeting. While accomplishing these tasks, you must demonstrate competence, empathy, sensitivity to differences in values and desires, and optimism.

Chapter 2
Understanding Child Management Skills

In this chapter, we describe seven basic child management skills. We devote three skills to increasing appropriate behavior — praise and attention, rewards and privileges, and suggestive praise — and four skills to decreasing inappropriate behavior — ignoring, time-out, removing rewards and privileges, and physical punishment. As we explain skills, we review what they have in common, spell out each technique in detail, highlight the most important aspects for parents to practice, and conclude with key points to remember.

SKILLS TO INCREASE APPROPRIATE BEHAVIOR

What the Skills Have in Common

Praise and attention, rewards and privileges, and suggestive praise are related by the common premise that parents can use positive consequences to increase their children's appropriate behavior. For all three skills, parents must learn to; (a) notice appropriate behavior, (b) practice diligently and apply the skills frequently, (c) direct their attention only to behavior they want to occur more often, and (d) individualize their use of the skills to fit each child's preferences. Even though we recommend specific procedures for skill use, we encourage all parents to employ the skills in ways that best fit their personal styles and their family's values.

We first teach parents positive skills because they are easier to apply consistently than is punishment and children are more receptive of parents new positive — rather than new punishing — behavior. When parents start using praise and attention, rewards and privileges, and suggestive praise, their children begin behaving more desirably. Parents learn they can have control in pleasant ways, and their attitudes about their parenting and their children improve: They have more motivation and opportunities to use the positive skills.

Some parents find it difficult to accept the idea that they can use positive consequences to help their children learn desirable behavior. We believe these parents are caught in a "discipline trap." They have come to the erroneous conclusion that "disciplining" is synonymous with "punishing" and that their children's disciplined behavior is derived solely from punishment. This error causes serious problems. When parents mistakenly learn they should teach discipline through punishment, they are often inconsistent. Whether the inconsistency derives from parents' reluctance to punish, or whether it comes from an inability to attend to all the behaviors they believe call for punishment, the results are virtually the same: They teach discipline ineffectively.

A brief visit to a laundromat, toy store, or supermarket will reveal parents' inconsistency using punishment to discipline their children. Patterson (1982) has found inconsistent punishment to be central in a family's coercive interaction patterns. Parents who have trouble because they punish their children inconsistently, also have problems because they have not learned how to teach and encourage as a method of discipline. When parents learn to use positive responses, however, they realize the joyful and rewarding aspects of teaching their children appropriate behavior. Parents also learn that discipline does not have to come from children's fear of punishment. Discipline can instead result from positive consequences for desirable behavior. Simply, parents can make their children feel good about behaving well.

The positive skills require that parents pay attention to appropriate behavior that usually passes unnoticed. For example, when a loud unruly child plays quietly, that is the perfect time for parents to use praise, rewards and privileges, or suggestive praise. At first, some parents find it difficult to give this attention. When their children behave well, they are relieved that there are no problems and hope the quiet, desirable behavior continues. They may even stay away from their well-behaved children, afraid their presence will upset the pleasant behavior. If parents do not use their positive skills when their children behave well and, instead, respond to their children for misbehaving, they create an escalating cycle of punishment and misbehavior that is sustained by parental attention.

A positive approach can stop this cycle. Parents can use their positive skills to teach children what to do: Parents do not have to reserve their efforts for stopping problems. Parents can be happier with their children, and their children will learn important living skills.

SKILL 1: PRAISE AND ATTENTION

The first skill, praise and attention, serves as the foundation for many subsequent skills. When parents master the use of praise and attention, they

Understanding Child Management Skills

also learn general concepts that are fundamental in performing other parenting skills. Most importantly, they learn that their attention can have powerful effects on their children's behavior. Parents discover how to use this powerful attention selectively, only during or immediately after behavior they want to occur more often.

Skill description. — Praise and attention includes positive statements, descriptions of behavior, touching, and physical affection.

Rationale for using praise and attention. — A variety of studies have demonstrated the effectiveness of praise and attention to change behavior. Researchers have shown that when parents follow their children's behavior with attention, the frequency of the behavior increases (Dubey and Kaufman, 1977; Herbert & Baer, 1972; Wahler, 1969). Other researchers found appropriate child behaviors increased when parents were specifically taught to describe aloud the desirable behavior their children were performing, and to follow the description with positive attention (Dangel & Polster, 1984; Forehand & King, 1977).

Parents find the following list of benefits useful to understand why they should use praise and attention:

1. Praise and attention teaches appropriate behavior, whereas punishment only teaches what not to do: it does not teach alternatives.
2. Praise and attention helps children feel good about themselves.
3. Praise and attention helps build harmonious family relationships.
4. When children try to learn something new, praise and attention can help their acquisition of new skills.

Practicing Praise and Attention

Our recommendations for skill practice instruct parents how to use praise and attention effectively.

Use praise and attention only during or immediately after behavior you want to happen more often. Parents maximize their praise and attention effectiveness when they use it at the correct time: while their children are behaving desirably. For example, Mr. Jackson used praise and attention at the right time when he praised his 7-year-old son, Gary. The boy answered the telephone. "Hello, Jacksons' residence, may I help you"? The caller asked, "May I speak to your father, please?" Gary responded, "Hold on, please," and then said to his father, "Dad, it's for you." Before Mr. Jackson spoke to the caller, he said to his son, "Gary, you answered the phone very politely. I really appreciate it." Mr. Jackson praised his son immediately for his polite telephone behavior. Chances are improved that Gary will also answer the phone politely in the future.

Withhold praise and attention when children misbehave. Even staring, glaring, sighing, and other subtle noises of exasperation (e.g., "tsk, tsk") can increase the behavior parents really want to eliminate.

Some parents express concern at withholding their attention when their children "sass" or disobey. Empathize with them when they insist they must try to stop misbehavior, and explain that you will be covering methods for stopping problems in future sessions. Reemphasize the point that any attention can increase any behavior, desirable as well as undesirable, so they must be careful with their attention. Recommend that they try to withhold their attention from behavior they do not want to occur more often, but if they absolutely cannot, they should rely on the methods they have used in the past.

Make your praise descriptive. When parents make their praise descriptive they accomplish two important tasks. First, their attention encourages their children to continue what they are doing. Second, their description helps their children learn what they should do to get positive attention again. Descriptive praise can include comments about a child's behavior such as, "Kenny, you sure look like you're having a good time playing with your toy gas station." Or descriptive praise can specify aspects of a task or game in which the child is involved, such as, "Doreen, you're brushing the dog and putting all his shed hair in the garbage pail."

Parents' first attempts to describe behavior are sometimes awkward and incomplete. Some individuals find it difficult to conceptualize behavior as a series of discrete events. Parents can improve their ability to praise when they learn to describe what their children are doing. Their descriptions are the foundation upon which they build more complete and effective praise statements.

Include positive comments and encouragement in your praise. Parents can make their plain descriptions into praise by adding content that commends their children's behavior. They can use these statements to evaluate positively a task or game in which their children are involved. For example, "Tammy, you're doing an excellent job on your math homework. Your numbers look neat and the columns all line up. It's so easy to read." Parents can also use positive comments to urge their children to continue what they are doing. Ms. Drummond encouraged her 10-year-old son to continue practicing the piano when she said, "You're playing has really been fine today, David. You've practiced for 30 minutes without stopping and almost every note sounded right. It sure seems like you'll have no trouble finishing your practice time today."

Give praise for minor appropriate behavior. A very difficult, but important, aspect of training parents to use praise is teaching them to identify and pay attention to the minor good things their children do each day. Many parents ignore their children for doing "what's expected of them," such as reading quietly, trying to tie shoelaces, using a fork appropriately, or limiting the duration of telephone calls. It is just at these times, when their children are doing something minor, but desirable, that parents should use their praise and attention.

Because it can be difficult for parents to begin praising minor behavior, emphasize the importance of this aspect of the skill. If parents wait for important behavior to occur before they give praise, they will have few instances to practice. Also, if parents rarely praise minor desirable behavior, their children will probably not perform these behaviors with any greater frequency. Increasing the minor behavior is so important because it is usually the many minor good behaviors, not the few major positive actions, that make the difference between parents who identify their children as well behaved and parents who claim their children, "never do anything right."

Make your praise sincere. Parents with limited experience in using praise or those who have extensive histories of problems with their children, may find it particularly tough to praise for behavior they have traditionally considered, "what their children are supposed to do." When parents respond to our explanation of praise with hesitance, regarding their ability to sincerely praise minor behavior, we point out that we do not want them to praise *all* behavior, but we want them to praise those behaviors they really do appreciate and want to happen again.

Some parents claim they cannot praise sincerely because their children are never "good." Encourage them to observe their children more often and in more situations. When parents increase the frequency and occasion of checking on their children, they usually learn that their children do many fine things during the day and there are, in fact, many behaviors that warrant praise and attention. Even after parents find more appropriate behavior, however, frequent praise is a new skill for them and they may not sound sincere. They must force themselves to use a pleasant voice tone and to avoid sarcasm, such as, "You made your bed, finally." or "Bob, you did your homework without my nagging. I can't believe it." When parents practice, they learn to praise sincerely.

Use physical affection with praise. Using physical affection with praise, or by itself, enhances parents' efforts at teaching their children appropriate behavior. Physical affection can include hugs, pats on the back, kisses, tickles, and any other physical demonstration of appreciation that parents know their children like.

Fit praise to each child's likes and dislikes. Some parents are quite familiar with the kinds of praise and attention their children prefer. Some children like hugs, other children like kisses, some prefer having their hair mussed and others hate it, and some enjoy hearing lavish praise, whereas other children are most pleased with a simple description or a short verbal acknowledgment. Some of these preferences are typical during certain age periods, such as adolescents preferring their parents not demonstrate affection toward them in public. Other preferences are highly individualized, such as a child's preference for a particular nickname. Effective parents use the kind of attention their children like best. Although many parents are well versed in their children's particular preferences, other parents know little of their children's likes and dislikes.

Parents can learn their children's preferences by using the kind of attention that is most comfortable for them and then observing their children's reactions. When children respond negatively, parents should refrain from using that type of attention. When children respond positively, parents must remember that form of attention as effective and try to use it again. Some children complain of embarrassment or discomfort when their parents first start using praise. When this happens, encourage parents to be particularly sensitive to their children's preferences for praise and attention. Parents learn, over time, that their children actually look forward to praise and behave well to deserve it. Caution parents, however, that if their children seem to be embarrassed when praised, they must try different kinds of attention until they discover the type their children like.

Vary praise each time you use it. Overused types of praise or attention, lose their impact. When children hear, "good girl," "good boy," or "well done" over and over, they soon ignore it. Parents can vary their praise and attention by changing the combinations of the skill components. Sometimes they can use just a few words of praise and encouragement, such as, "Janet, you're doing a fine job brushing Princess. I bet she likes that." Other times, parents can use more elaborate praises, such as, "You sure look like you enjoy that finger painting, Shanika. Its so nice that you try to express yourself in art. The colors you're using are very pretty and the shapes you're making look beautiful. I like your picture."

Encourage and praise parents' skill practice. If we fail to recognize parents' efforts or forget to emphasize the importance of frequent skill practice, their efforts soon diminish. Your attention to parents' work can prevent this. When you help parents to use praise and attention consistently, their children's behavior will improve and they will have even more opportunities and reasons to use it.

Key Points to Remember About Praise and Attention
1. Use praise and attention only during or immediately after behavior you want to happen more often.
2. Withhold praise and attention when children misbehave.
3. Make your praise descriptive.
4. Include positive comments and encouragement in your praise.
5. Give praise for minor appropriate behavior.
6. Make your praise sincere.
7. Use physical affection with praise.
8. Fit praise to each child's likes and dislikes.
9. Vary praise each time you use it.

SKILL 2: REWARDS AND PRIVILEGES

Skill description. Rewards and privileges are explicit consequences for specific behavior. Consequences can include everything from extra time with mom, to a special activity, and from an item of clothing to a toy. Sometimes the consequences are specified before the behavior; sometimes after.

Rationale for using rewards and privileges. Many studies show that rewards and privileges change behavior. Researchers have demonstrated that even simple, inexpensive rewards increase the behavior they follow. Parents have effectively changed their children's behavior by using a variety of low-cost and naturally occurring rewards and privileges, such as sharing parents' free time (Dangel & Polster, 1984), nickels (Bach & Moyland, 1975), food (Ayllon & Roberts, 1975), late bedtime (Hall, 1984), and access to television, telephone, and free time (Polster and Pinkston, 1979).

Rewards and privileges help parents increase their options for individualizing their positive attention. In fact, parents use rewards and privileges as another variation of positive attention for their children's desirable behavior. Rewards and privileges are as effective as praise and attention for increasing desirable behavior.

When parents advance to this skill they have already seen positive results from using praise and attention, and they are ready to learn how to enhance their effectiveness.

Parents find the following list of benefits useful to understand why they should use rewards and privileges:

1. Rewards and privileges show, in ways your children can understand, that you are pleased with their behavior and that you would like them to continue what they are doing.
2. You already do dozens of nice things for your children each day. You can effectively use these things as rewards and privileges.
3. When your children accomplish something that has been extra difficult for them, a special reward or privilege can express your pleasure.
4. When you reward your children you help them feel good about themselves and encourage them to try again.
5. Sometimes, you can use the promise of a reward or privilege as an incentive to perform desirable behavior.

Practicing Rewards and Privileges

Effective reward and privilege use shares commonalities with the methods of praise and attention. Parents use both skills during or immediately after a behavior they want to happen more often. Both skills include descriptions of behavior, positive comments and encouragement, and physical affection. In addition to these particulars, rewards and privileges require parents to use the many positive things they already do for their children as consequences for desirable behavior. Effective skill use requires that parents, (a) vary and individualize rewards and privileges, (b) match the size of the rewards and privileges to the importance or difficulty of a specific behavior, and (c) occasionally inform children ahead of time what they can do to earn a reward or privilege.

Present rewards and privileges only during or immediately after desired behavior. As with praise and attention, the timing of rewards and privileges is crucial. Parents present rewards and privileges only during or immediately after behavior they want to happen more often. Do not make the mistake of giving a reward before a performance. This problem was demonstrated in the Chan family. Sara Chan was vacuuming the living room rug when her mother entered the room. The girl stopped vacuuming and asked her mother for money to play video games. Her mother told her that she could not have any money until she finished cleaning. Sara responded, "But, Mom, Jill and Ariel are waiting for me and I promised I'd be there in 10 minutes and that was 20 minutes ago." Ms. Chan could not resist the desperation Sara had in her voice and replied, "Okay, here's two quarters for the games, but from now on you have to finish your chores first." Sara left to meet her friends and Ms.

Chan finished the vacuuming. She inadvertently taught her daughter that she could arrange things to get out of work and get an early reward.

Do not use rewards and privileges to stop misbehavior. We call this bribery. This inappropriate use of rewards and privileges often teaches children they should misbehave so they can earn a reward for stopping. Mr. Blakenship used bribery at his friend's house when his 4-year-old daughter, Penny, walked on the couch.

The embarrassed father told the girl, "Penny, you know you're not supposed to walk on furniture. Now get down." The girl just laughed and continued to stand on the couch. Mr. Blakenship just got more embarrassed and bribed his daughter, "If you get off the couch I'll give you a nickel." The girl got off the couch and her father paid her. The embarrassed father taught his little girl that if she wants to earn some bribery money, all she has to do is refuse to stop misbehaving.

Accompany rewards and privileges with descriptions of the rewarded behavior. Describing behavior, one of the primary skills parents learned for praise and attention, is also fundamental in using rewards and privileges. Rewards show children their parents are pleased with their behavior, but descriptions specify what they did to earn the reward. Parents' descriptions help children learn how to behave in the future to make rewards and privileges more likely.

Use positive and encouraging words when giving rewards and privileges. When praise accompanies rewards, both the praise and the reward can have an increased effect: They boost each other. As in praise and attention, positive and encouraging words can help children feel good about themselves and learn what to do for positive attention. When children receive rewards and privileges with praise, they have additional evidence of their parents' pleasure and something tangible to enjoy as the "fruits of their labor."

Parents should use the nice things they already do as rewards and privileges. Many parents do not realize that each day they give their children many rewards and privileges without any prerequisites for desirable behavior. These parents do not seem to appreciate that it is their own hard work and generosity that make many privileges, comforts, and material possessions available to their children. Comfortable beds, televisions, stereos, parents' free time, favorite desserts, late bedtimes, clothes, and the opportunity to make choices regarding anything from which television program the family will watch to whether to have cornflakes or eggs for breakfast, are just a few examples of rewards and privileges that parents give their children each day, often without regard to the children's behavior. Try to help parents stop letting their children "freeload" and start requiring desirable behavior for access to rewards and privileges.

Parents can start using the nice, everyday things they do as rewards simply by informing their children when a contingency exists between a behavior and its consequence. For example, before learning about rewards and privileges, when Ms. Saltzmann's children arrived at the kitchen table she regularly asked them what they wanted for breakfast. Sometimes the kids got to the table so close to their school departure time they would not have time to finish their meal. After Ms. Saltzmann learned she could use everyday privileges to impact behavior, she changed her morning routine. The next morning her children arrived at the table with plenty of time to eat so she told them, "Since you got to breakfast on time, you can choose between cereal and eggs." Ms. Saltzmann began teaching her children that having a choice of food is a reward they can earn. If her children arrived late to breakfast she simply served the food she thought they had time to finish and gave them no choice.

Vary rewards and privileges each time you use them. It is common for parents to find that items or activities which their children find rewarding one time have little or no value at another time. Parents can avoid this problem by learning a variety of consequences their children desire and by offering alternatives.

There are many ways to vary rewards and privileges. First, parents can use the many positive things they do and the opportunities they make available as an extensive menu of possible rewards and privileges. They can also vary rewards and privileges by changing their style of presentation. For example, one time they can accompany a reward with physical affection and another time they can use positive words with a privilege. In any case, they should individualize their style for their children's likes and dislikes. When parents consistently tailor rewards and privileges to fit the importance of behavior and their children's desires, they will naturally vary their skill use.

Individualize rewards and privileges for children's likes and dislikes. Parents can use anything their children like as rewards and privileges. They must, of course, discontinue offering rewards or privileges their children do not like. This may seem obvious, but there are some parents who have continued to offer rewards they thought their children *should* like, even though the children never expressed positive reactions to them. Some noneffective "rewards" have been, cookies, TV time, going to the movies, and a puppy.

Some children respond best to being given more free time, others like to spend more time with their parents. When children do not respond positively to particular rewards, parents should watch their children closely during free time to identify the kinds of things they like. Parents can also ask their children to identify rewards or privileges they would like.

Sometimes parents offer a reward and their children request a different one. If this does not happen often, and the requested substitution is acceptable to the parents, this is fine. This type of substitution can be another way for parents to individualize their rewards and to learn more about what their children desire.

Regardless of how parents learn what their children want, effective rewards and privileges do not have to be expensive or outstanding. Some parents are surprised to find their children have rather modest tastes and can be rewarded inexpensively. Many parents are pleased to discover that their children consider spending time with them to be a valuable reward.

Give rewards and privileges in proportion to the importance and difficulty of behavior. Parents must work out this proportion for individual circumstances according to the specific value they place on certain behavior and relative to other things their children do. For example, a child who has a history of severe aggressiveness should get a more significant reward for playing well with others than for a clean room.

Occasionally tell children ahead of time what they can do to earn rewards and privileges. When parents tell their children how they can earn a reward or privilege they accomplish three things at once. First, if children know what they must do in order to get something they want, they are encouraged to behave well in the future. Second, parents can encourage their children to continue present desirable behavior with statements such as, "If you continue to play quietly with your sister, I'll take you both to the park this afternoon." Third, when parents tell their children how they can earn a reward or privilege, they also teach them to be independent and responsible. The children are required to take it upon themselves to perform appropriately and on time. For example, Mr. Jefferson told his 10-year-old daughter, Lenore, "If you help me by cleaning out the car this afternoon, I'll drive you over to Crosby's Cycle Shop to pick up your bike. Let me know when you're finished."

It is important that when parents promise their children opportunities to earn rewards for good behavior, they follow through on their agreement. On one of our home visits we observed a parent not following through. Twelve-year-old William came into the room, excused himself, and said, "Mom, I finished dusting the blinds in the living room, now can you take me to the hobby store when your meeting is over?" Ms. Minoso responded, "Oh, Billy, I forgot I promised to take Grandma to the grocery store, we'll go later in the week, okay?" William angrily replied "You promised! I'm not going to do anything you ask anymore!" and he left the room. Ms. Minoso showed William she does not keep her word and he will be less likely to comply with his mother's requests in the future.

When some children learn their parents will set the opportunity for earning rewards, they try to negotiate rewards for all their behavior. Parents must assess whether the requests are from avarice or from a general lack of rewards. If there are few rewards, parents should increase the frequency. If the requests represent an unquenchable desire for material acquisition, and the parents find this undesirable, the parents should explain that rewards and privileges will be delivered and offered when the parents think they are deserved. They should also explain that if the children persist in their requesting or haggling for constant rewards, they will get nothing they ask for.

Key Points to Remember About Rewards and Privileges.
1. Present rewards and privileges only during or immediately after desired behavior.
2. Do not use rewards and privileges to stop misbehavior.
3. Accompany rewards and privileges with descriptions of the rewarded behavior.
4. Use positive and encouraging words when giving rewards and privileges.
5. Physical affection should often accompany rewards and privileges.
6. Parents should use the nice things they already do as rewards and privileges.
7. Rewards and privileges should vary each time they are used.
8. Individualize rewards and privileges for children's likes and dislikes.
9. Give rewards and privileges in proportion to the importance and difficulty of behavior.
10. Occasionally tell children ahead of time what they can do to earn rewards and privileges.

SKILL 3: SUGGESTIVE PRAISE

Skill description. Suggestive praise commends children for *not* misbehaving. It reminds them of what they are doing appropriately and what misbehavior they are avoiding. Suggestive praise statements use words such as, "for not," "instead of," or "without." Examples of suggestive praise include: "Thank you *for not* leaving your dishes on the table,". "Great! you closed the door quietly *instead of* slamming it"; and "Jill, you're tying your shoes *without* my help."

Rationale for using suggestive praise. Suggestive praise is more commonly known in the literature as differential reinforcement of other behavior, or

DRO. Researchers have taught parents to use suggestive praise to stop problematic behavior by attending to a desirable behavior that was incompatible with the problem. Through DRO, parents have learned how to: reduce sibling conflicts (Leitenberg, Burchard, Burchard, Fuller, & Lysaught, 1977), decrease thumbsucking (Knight & McKenzie, 1974), alleviate the severity of asthma (Neisworth & Moore, 1972), diminish nagging and whining (Dangel & Polster, 1984), and curb temper tantrums (Pinkston, Friedman, & Polster, 1981).

Parents find the following list of benefits useful to understand why they should use suggestive praise:

1. Suggestive praise can stop problems before they start or become serious.
2. Suggestive praise helps parents teach their children, in positive ways, what they should not do.
3. Suggestive praise adds to the parents' repertoire of positive skills for teaching desirable behavior.
4. Suggestive praise encourages children to continue behaving desirably.

Practicing Suggestive Praise

Suggestive praise means a new challenge for you and the parents with whom you work. This is the first child management skill that most parents have never tried. If you have been encouraging the parents and they have been practicing, they have become proficient at giving praise and attention and rewards and privileges during or immediately after their children's desirable behavior. Parents' proficiency is important because, starting with suggestive praise, the skills become more difficult: They require more discrimination and thoughtfulness. Suggestive praise is particularly important for those parents who claim their children "never do anything I can praise or reward." With suggestive praise, parents have little reason for infrequent skill use — their children are not constantly misbehaving. When parents learn that suggestive praise is used to decrease undesirable behavior as well as to increase the desirable, they try to work harder at practicing the skill and they find many opportunities to use it when their children are not misbehaving.

There are important similarities between suggestive praise, rewards and privileges, and praise and attention. As parents have learned the importance of timing in the previous skills, they should learn to use suggestive praise only during or immediately after behavior they want to occur more often. Additional ways in which suggestive praise is similar to rewards and privileges and praise and attention are: (a) parents must use descriptive and sincere statements; (b) parents should vary and individualize their suggestive praise each time they use it by combining positive words, physical affection, and rewards and privileges with suggestive praise statements.

Suggestive praise requires phrases such as "for not," "instead of," or "without." Parents use these phrases to remind their children of the misbehavior they are avoiding. Examples of suggestive praise statements include: "You put your toys away and got ready for bed *without* complaining"; "You ate an apple *instead of* a piece of cake"; and "Thank you *for not* whining when I said we couldn't go swimming this afternoon." Each of the three examples demonstrates parents using suggestive praise when their children were behaving well in situations that had typically been problematic.

Suggestive praise should be given when children are not misbehaving. Parents can accomplish this in one of two ways. First, they simply have to notice when their children do not perform in a typically problematic way. For example, Mr. Collins' 11-year-old daughter, Shalimar, often used the telephone for extended durations. One evening the girl hung up the telephone after a relatively short conversation and Mr. Collins said, "Shalimar, you got off the phone after only five minutes instead of an hour. Thanks a lot."

Parents can also use suggestive praise at the correct time by identifying situations in which their children frequently misbehave. Parents check on their children when they are in these typically problematic situations and use suggestive praise when they find their children are not misbehaving. For example, Ms. Rivas' twin sons often fought with each other during play times. When she checked on the boys and found them getting along well, she used suggestive praise: "Jimmy and Joey, it's great the way you two are playing so well together without fighting."

You can help parents use suggestive praise at the most appropriate times by explaining that their children often perform desirable behavior immediately preceding undesirable behavior. For example: siblings may play well together just before they start a fight, a child might use watercolors neatly on paper preceding painting on a dining room table, or a child may ask politely for assistance with a chore before escalating to screaming and demanding. In any case, for parents to use suggestive praise at the best time, they must use it for the desirable behavior *before* the misbehavior occurs.

Suggestive praise must be descriptive. Effective suggestive praise statements inform children what they *are not* doing that pleases their parents. If parents are not descriptive, their children will not recognize the desirable behavior they performed, and the suggestive praise will not decrease the problem behavior. Ms. Washington was not descriptive when she told her 6-year-old daughter Constance, "Connie, you're eating okay. You aren't doing it like you used to." Connie probably had no idea what her mother was talking about. The correct way for the mother to have used suggestive praise would have included a description such as, "Connie, you're using your knife and fork to cut your meat instead of putting extra-big pieces in your mouth."

Suggestive praise must be sincere. When there are serious, or long-standing problems, parents can be annoyed with their children, and may find it difficult to be sincere when they praise them for not performing a problem behavior. For example, 7-year-old Eugene often spilled his milk when he poured it for himself at dinner. When Mr. Osborne tried to use suggestive praise for Eugene not spilling his milk, the father's statement hardly sounded like praise: "Eugene, you poured your milk without spilling it, it's about time you stopped being so clumsy." We explained to the father that the way he responded to his son's success sounded more like criticism than praise. A more positive and sincere suggestive praise would have been, "Eugene, you poured that milk without getting a drop on the table!"

Sometimes combine suggestive praise with praise and attention. Suggestive praise helps increase desirable behavior by incorporating positive and encouraging words for it. Parents should have mastered this skill component during praise and attention. An example of suggestive praise that incorporates positive words would be, "Jenny, you did a beautiful job tying your hair back, instead of letting it hang in your face. It looks wonderful." An example of suggestive praise that includes encouraging words would be, "Sonny, you're doing your homework without watching television; I bet you'll do a great job on it!"

Sometimes combine suggestive praise with physical affection. Parents can use physical affection to dramatize their pleasure that their children *are not* behaving problematically. For example, Mr. Winter's 8-year-old daughter, Becky, often whined whenever her father refused to grant a request. The father decided that whenever Becky accepted his decision without whining, he would use suggestive praise. The next morning at breakfast, Becky asked her father if she could have pancakes. Mr. Winter replied that there was no time to prepare pancakes. Becky simply responded, "Okay, I'll just have cereal." The father was pleased that Becky did not whine. He gave her a hug and said, "Becky, thank you for not whining when I said you couldn't have pancakes for breakfast." Becky hugged her father back and said, "That's okay, Daddy." Parents should be familiar with and use the kinds of physical affection their children favor.

Sometimes include rewards and privileges with suggestive praise. When parents are particularly pleased that their children are not performing a problem behavior and are behaving well, they can pair a reward or privilege with their suggestive praise. For example Mr. Dunston noticed his 10-year-old son, Richie, preparing a messy science project on the floor of the garage. He used suggestive praise and rewarded Richie, "Son, for not bringing that project inside and messing up the house, you can choose the movie that we're going to see tonight."

Suggestive praise should be individualized. Whether parents give suggestive praise by itself, or add physical affection or rewards and privileges to it, they must tailor their praise statements to fit their children. Just as with praise and attention, parents should not use suggestive praise with a 12-year-old the same way they would present it to a 5-year-old. Parents will have to experiment with suggestive praise to find how it works best. Ms. Cody was ineffective with her suggestive praise when she used complex words with her 5-year-old daughter. On a home visit, we watched Ms. Cody's daughter, Gina, ask her mother if she could play outside. Ms. Cody told her daughter she couldn't go out just then, but perhaps she could go out "when the two doctors leave." Gina looked at us and said, "Okay, I'll wait." Ms. Cody responded, "Thank you, Gina, for not being tenacious." After we recovered from our surprise at the vocabulary Ms. Cody directed at her 5-year-old, we asked Gina if she could tell us what her mother just said to her. Gina replied, "Mommy said thank you because I wasn't 'abashus'." All of us, including Ms. Cody, broke into laughter at Gina's interpretation of her mother's suggestive praise. Ms. Cody did not require any additional coaching from us to point out that she needed to individualize her suggestive praises for Gina's intellectual level. When we quieted down, Ms. Cody told Gina, "I'm sorry, honey, what I meant to say was, 'Thank you for not nagging.' I like it when you and I are friendly." She then gave her daughter a big hug. We discussed the incident with the mother and gave her the opportunity to practice a few more individualized suggestive praises.

Vary suggestive praise each time you use it. Parents can devise variations by changing the words they use, and by occasionally using suggestive praise in combination with the other skills, such as, rewards, physical affection, and positive words. For example, 4-year-old Julianna was usually hesitant to try new foods at dinner. Often, before Julie even got the new food to her lips, she would make a face of disgust and sometimes hold her nose. Her parents started using suggestive praise with Julie when she tried a new food without any fuss. At one meal, Julie's mother noticed her trying romaine lettuce for the first time. As Julie was putting the first bite in her mouth her mother said, "Julianna, you're really a brave girl to try that lettuce without making a face." In this example, the parent used positive words with suggestive praise. The parents offered Julie boiled potatoes. Her father watched closely, and as

Juliana put her fork into a potato he said, "Julie, after you try that potato without holding your nose, you can decide whether we go for a bike ride or play tag after dinner." By varying their suggestive praise, Julie's parents had a greater impact on reducing their daughter's finicky eating.

Key Points to Remember About Suggestive Praise
1. Suggestive praise requires phrases such as "for not," "instead of," or "without."
2. Suggestive praise should be given when children are not misbehaving.
3. Suggestive praise must be descriptive.
4. Suggestive praise must be sincere.
5. Sometimes combine suggestive praise with praise and attention.
6. Sometimes combine suggestive praise with physical affection.
7. Sometimes include rewards and privileges with suggestive praise.
8. Suggestive praise should be individualized.
9. Vary suggestive praise each time you use it.

SKILLS TO DECREASE INAPPROPRIATE BEHAVIOR

What the Skills Have in Common

Ignoring, time-out, removing rewards and privileges, and physical punishment are skills we teach to decrease inappropriate behavior. These skills are related by the common premise that parents can use negative consequences to decrease their children's inappropriate behavior. They provide alternatives to other less effective or more punitive methods to decrease inappropriate behavior.

Even though the skills we teach for decreasing inappropriate behavior are more effective and less punitive than some other methods of child management, it is critical that you remind parents that the three positive methods for increasing behavior should be the skills they rely on to teach their children appropriate behavior. Some parents, particularly those whose children have been problematic for a long time, may mistakenly emphasize punishment as a means to eliminate problems, rather than depend on positive consequences to increase the desirable things their children do. Parents need to know they do not teach their children what *to do* when they use punishment: Positive consequences do this. Punishment only teaches children what *not* to do. Parents should use the skills for decreasing inappropriate behavior so they will have more opportunity to use the positive skills.

Most children will occasionally behave in ways their parents dislike. We have yet to meet the "perfect" child and we believe we would rather not. The always-perfect child would likely be quite boring – if such a child existed. Since there really is no absolute standard for correct child behavior, we encourage parents to determine for themselves which of their children's undesirable behaviors they identify as serious, dangerous, or absolutely intolerable.

All the skills in this section are designed to decrease inappropriate behavior, but one skill, *ignoring*, is used primarily to handle minor annoyances, such as whining or nagging. The other skills, *time-out*, *removing rewards and privileges*, and *physical punishment* are used for serious problems. We discuss ignoring first.

SKILL 4: IGNORING

Ignoring is the least intrusive but probably *the most difficult skill* we teach parents. Often, when parents have had ongoing problems with their children, they may believe they have tried virtually everything to try to get the problems to stop. For parents with a particularly active history of intervention attempts, ignoring can be a foreign concept and a difficult skill to learn.

Even though ignoring may initially sound alien to some parents, we do, in fact, introduce it in all the positive skills. In the first lesson we tell parents to withhold their attention until their children perform behavior they want to happen more often. In the second lesson we explain that parents should not give rewards or privileges while their children are misbehaving. In the third lesson we teach parents to wait (ignore) until their children are not performing a problem behavior before they use suggestive praise. The basic idea in ignoring is for parents to withhold their attention from *all* behavior they want to stop and to respond only to those behaviors they want to happen more often. Ignoring is a skill parents must master to maximize the impact of their positive attention.

Skill description. Ignoring is the systematic withholding of attention following some minor annoying or aggravating behavior.

Rationale for using ignoring. Many studies have shown the effectiveness of ignoring, technically known as *extinction* for decreasing problem behavior. Williams (1959), in a classic study, taught parents to effectively ignore their infant's inappropriate crying at bedtime. Hall (1984), in another study, used "planned ignoring" in her Responsive Parenting program to successfully reduce uncooperative whining and crying. McMahon and Forehand (1984) taught parents to employ ignoring to effectively decrease their children's noncompliance with a variety of parental requests and directions.

Parents find the following list of benefits useful to understand why they should use ignoring:

1. Ignoring is not the same as doing nothing. It is a difficult method of discipline that requires a great deal of control and consistency on your part.
2. Ignoring is a very effective method to teach your children which of their behaviors will *not* get your attention.
3. When you ignore a bothersome behavior, you discourage your children from performing it again.
4. Ignoring is just one skill for decreasing problems. Later lessons teach additional methods that stop serious or dangerous behavior.

Practicing Ignoring

Whenever your children are doing something that seems to be for your attention and you would like them to stop, ignore them.

Some examples of these annoying, attention-seeking behaviors include whining, nagging, tattling, and pouting.

Ignoring annoying behavior can be extremely difficult. The most difficult aspect of the skill generally stems from the necessity that parents consistently and completely ignore the bothersome behavior. This means no glaring, no staring, no warnings — no attention of any kind. Some parents, who believe they are practicing ignoring, make the mistake of using "subtle" signs of displeasure in response to their children's misbehavior. They might, for example, make a deep sigh, say the child's name in a gruff tone, or shake their head. These responses are in fact attention and can serve to increase, rather than decrease, problematic behavior.

Use ignoring each time the bothersome behavior occurs. If parents ignore a behavior only sometimes, they may accidentally teach their children that if they perform the problem behavior often enough it will eventually get their parent's attention. This intermittent attention serves to make a behavior stronger, not weaker. The parent's inconsistency in ignoring teaches the children to perform a behavior for long periods of time between episodes of attention: Children learn to tolerate intermittent ignoring. Children's nagging and whining are good examples of bothersome behavior that, if ignored inconsistently, often escalates to intolerable levels. When the whining or nagging reaches new decibel levels and parents consequently respond, they teach their children to nag or whine at the new (improved), more effective, severity.

When you ignore a problem, it may get worse before it gets better. If children have been regularly getting attention for a misbehavior, it will not decrease as soon as the parent starts ignoring it. The problem took some time to develop; it will take time to diminish. If parents cannot tolerate a temporary increase in the misbehavior, it may be better for them to continue responding to the problem in the ways they have in the past. They should wait until they learn other skills for decreasing behavior before they try to solve the problem.

Do something distracting to help you ignore. Ignoring can be very difficult when a child is behaving obnoxiously. Counting to ten, talking to a spouse, or leaving the room can help parents learn to completely and consistently ignore their children's annoying behavior. All parents will need to develop their own strategy for distracting themselves.

Use suggestive praise with ignoring. Ignoring is easier and more effective when parents combine it with suggestive praise. The first step in this process is to totally ignore the child's annoying behavior. After the annoying behavior stops, the parent should wait briefly and then use suggestive praise. Parents should mention the ignored behavior in the suggestive praise statement. If, for example, at the dinner table 6-year-old Jimmy was pushing the peas around his plate with his fork, his father should ignore him until he stops. The father should wait briefly, until Jimmy behaves appropriately, and then he should make a suggestive praise statement such as, "Jimmy, you're eating your peas correctly instead of pushing them around your plate. That's great!"

Sometimes, ignoring may not be the best method of discipline for a parent to use. If a child is doing something dangerous, like hitting, refusing parental requests, or something else that a parent cannot tolerate, perhaps some form of punishment, which is covered in the following skill lessons, may be more appropriate.

Key Points to Remember About Ignoring
1. Whenever your children are doing something that seems to be for your attention and you would like them to stop, ignore them.
2. Use ignoring each time the bothersome behavior occurs.
3. When you ignore a problem, it may get worse before it gets better.
4. Do something distracting to help you ignore.
5. Use suggestive praise with ignoring.

SKILL 5: TIME-OUT

Time-out is the first skill we teach parents that focuses on stopping serious misbehavior. Time-out does not change our overall emphasis. We encourage parents to attend to the desirable behavior with praise and attention, rewards and privileges, and suggestive praise, and to use ignoring for annoying behavior they want their children to stop.

Keep parents' approaches positive by emphasizing the fundamental point that parents must reserve punishment, such as time-out, for serious, dangerous, or intolerable behavior. If children's behavior does not fit any of these categories, explain that ignoring is the most appropriate and effective parental response.

Skill description. Time-out involves making a child spend a few minutes in a corner or some other dull area where the child cannot find anything amusing or stimulating to do.

Rationale for time-out. Researchers have taught parents to use time-out for a variety of behaviors. In one example, 'Wahler (1969) trained parents to use time-out for their 5-year-old's oppositional behavior. In another project, Christophersen, Barrish, Barrish, and Christophersen (1984) taught parents to use time-out for general behavior problems. Pinkston (1984) trained parents to use time-out successfully to reduce their 6-year-old son's temper tantrums.

Parents find the following list of benefits useful to understand why they should use time-out:

1. When your children do something that is dangerous to themselves or to others, or behave in a way that you absolutely cannot tolerate, ignoring or suggestive praise may not be the best way to diminish such problems. Another way to reduce such behavior problems is to use time-out.
2. Time-out is an effective method of punishment that can teach your children what they must not do.
3. Time-out is immediate and brief. You can stop a problematic behavior, deliver a consequence that discourages your children from doing that behavior again, and terminate the punishment in a few minutes. Time-out's qualities of convenience and speed can help you be more consistent in your punishments and allow you to return to a more positive note.
4. Time-out is more humane than some other types of punishment, particularly spanking. You and your children will get less emotionally upset with the punishment, and with each other, when you use time-out rather than harsher methods.

Practicing Time-Out

Use time-out to decrease dangerous or serious problems. When parents have identified behavior as seriously problematic, dangerous, or something they absolutely cannot tolerate, time-out can reduce the problems. Some examples of behavior for which parents use time-out include: fighting, talking back, destroying property, not following important instructions, and throwing food when at the dinner table. Parents decide for themselves which behaviors they must try to stop immediately by using time-out.

Time-out involves making children spend a short period of time in a corner or other area especially arranged for it. Many places can be designated as appropriate time-out areas. Any place that will not give children an opportunity to entertain themselves will work. Parents should be careful *not* to use time-out areas that allow their children to face out of a window, look at pictures on a wall, or stand in front of manipulable objects.

Always use a dull area for time-out. In one instance a parent made her daughter sit on a stool facing a corner in the bathroom. In another example, a father had his son stand facing a wall in the hallway of their apartment. Parents generally select the most convenient, nonentertaining area they can find. At no time, however, should parents simply send their children to their bedroom for time-out.

Many parents have made the mistake of using their children's own room as a time-out area. The first problem with using children's bedrooms for time-out is that there are often many available distractions, such as toys and games. Time-out will not really be a punishment and, therefore, will not stop the problem behavior. The second problem with using children's rooms for punishment is that children should consider their room a positive place to go. If children begin to associate their rooms with punishment or other unpleasant circumstances, parents may find themselves having quite a bit of difficulty at bedtime trying to get their children to go to bed agreeably.

Use time-out only during or immediately after the behavior you want to decrease. For time-out to stop a specific behavior, parents must use it while the behavior is occurring. The longer the duration between problem behavior and time-out, the less likely a child will make a direct connection between time-out and the particular behavior for which it was used. For greatest time-out effectiveness, stop problematic behavior as soon as possible.

After a child starts a misbehavior, parents' first step is to grab the child firmly by the upper arm. They should not, of course, squeeze so hard as to hurt the child, but they should grasp strongly enough to let the child know there is a serious problem, and also to be able to retain the grip if the child tries to shake the hand off and run away. The parents' firm grip will cause two important things to happen. First, the misbehavior is stopped. Second, the parents get their children's attention.

Keep attention to a minimum during time-out. Once parents have a firm grip on their child's arm, they should make a clear, short statement about the problem behavior. This step should really occur simultaneously with grabbing the child's arm firmly. The statement must be terse in content, stern in tone, and informative. For example, Ms. Bledsoe saw her 7-year-old son hitting his sister. She grabbed him by the arm, stopping his hitting, and said, "You cannot hit your sister. Because you hit her, you will have to go to time-out." The woman was careful not to discuss the hitting any further with the child, regardless of what he said. Any additional conversation might actually have been positive attention for the child and time-out would have lost its impact.

Children should be kept in time-out briefly. The amount of time children should spend in time-out can vary, but it must always be brief. *Three to 5 minutes is sufficient.* When children are left in time-out for any longer than 5 minutes, they will find something to amuse themselves, regardless of how dreary the time-out area appears. Some children, for example, pick the paint off walls, others count the dots on wallpaper, and some children, who are particularly relaxed, go to sleep!

Another advantage of brief time-out is that parents are less likely to get busy with something and forget to end the punishment in a timely fashion. By keeping time-out brief, parents can easily be sure their isolated child is safe and out of mischief.

Sometimes parents can tell the duration of time-out to their children. Once they have a firm hold on the child's upper arm and describe the problem behavior, they can then state the duration for time-out. For example, Mr. Dunston found his 5-year-old daughter, Shelly, standing on a precarious stack of books in the kitchen trying to get another piece of chocolate cake off the top of the refrigerator. He had already told her she could not have cake before supper. He implemented time-out by setting Shelly carefully on the floor. As the father was letting the child down he sternly said, "Shelly, climbing on a pile of books that way is very dangerous. Also, you know you're not to have any more cake until after dinner tonight. Because what you were doing was dangerous *and* not allowed, you will have to be in time-out for 4 minutes." He then placed the girl in a chair facing the wall in the kitchen.

When the duration for time-out is complete, parents should tell their children their time is up and that they can return to an appropriate activity. It is very important that parents keep track of how long their children spend in time-out and be punctual about releasing them. Some parents find it helpful to use a kitchen timer to help them end time out promptly. They set the timer when time-out begins and tell their child the duration is complete when the timer bell rings. Regardless of how parents mark time, the statement that time-out is complete should be brief. For example, Ms. Blake told her son, "Mickey, your 3 minutes in time-out are over, you can go out and play again."

Sometimes it may take a while for a child to calm down in time-out. Some children make wisecracks, cry, complain, whine, or kick the wall they are facing. When this happens, parents should explain that their time does not start until they are quiet.

They should say nothing else. In some cases, children leave time-out before their time is complete. Parents should remain calm and return the child to time-out. When the child is back in the time-out area, parents should say, "Your time starts when you're sitting still (or standing still) and quiet." *They should say nothing else.*

Praise children for their first desirable behavior after time-out. Time-out works best when parents praise the behavior they want to happen more often. By using praise after time-out, parents show their children how to get attention for behaving in appropriate ways. When parents do not use their positive skills in addition to time-out, they often teach their children to misbehave. The only attention the children get, after all, is time-out for their undesirable behavior.

Parents can teach appropriate behavior after time-out by explaining why time-out was necessary and then praising the appropriate behavior as soon as it occurs. For example, when Joe's five minutes were complete, his father told him, "Joe, your time in time-out is over now. I want to remind you that I had to put you in time-out because you started screaming at me when I told you for the second time to stop playing with the cat and get ready for bed. I want you to get ready for bed the first time I tell you it's bedtime, with no backtalking and especially no shouting. Now, it's bedtime, get ready for bed." Joe said, "Okay," and went on to the bathroom to start his bedtime routine. His father followed Joe and when he got to the bathroom door the man said, "Joe, you started to get ready for bed without an argument; that's great. I appreciate it when we can cooperate with each other."

When parents use time-out they must not give the child a lot of attention for misbehaving. Some parents make the mistake of apologizing for implementing time-out. They say such things as, "I'm sorry to have to do this to you, sweetheart, but I'm afraid I have to put you in time-out," or "I know you don't like time-out, but you only have to stay there for a short time." These kinds of statements may cause children to associate positive experiences with time-out and it will not stop misbehavior.

Key Points to Remember About Time-Out
1. Use time-out to decrease dangerous or serious problems.

2. Always use a dull area for time-out.
3. Use time-out only during or immediately after the behaviour you want to decrease.
4. Keep attention to a minimum during time-out.
5. Children should be kept in time-out briefly.
6. Praise children for the first desirable thing they do after time-out.

SKILL 6: WITHDRAWING REWARDS AND PRIVILEGES

Withdrawing rewards and privileges is another method for stopping serious misbehavior. This skill incorporates many of the principles from an earlier lesson, Skill 2: Rewards and Privileges. In that lesson, parents learned to use the positive things they do each day to increase behavior. In this skill, however, parents withdraw the positive things, instead of presenting them, in order to decrease, rather than increase, behavior.

Skill description. Withdrawing rewards and privileges is defined as removing an opportunity, activity, privilege, or tangible item the child desires, in response to some dangerous, serious, or intolerable behavior.

Rationale for using the withdrawal of rewards and privileges. Many researchers have used successfully the withdrawal of rewards and privileges, referred to in the literature as "response cost," to reduce behavior problems. Holland (1969) helped parents eliminate their 7-year-old son's fire-setting behavior. The parents used the boy's "prized baseball glove" as the reward to be removed if he started another fire. In another example, Greene, Clark, and Risley (1977) required parents to remove rewards and privileges to help their children learn desirable behavior during family shopping trips. Patterson, Reid, Jones, and Conger (1975) helped parents arrange a home-based system in which the parents took away privileges, such as late bedtimes and television viewing time, when their children acted out.

Parents find the following list of benefits useful to understand why they should withdraw rewards and privileges:
1. At times your children may do something that is dangerous to themselves or to others, something serious, or absolutely intolerable. Even though you may prefer not to use punishment, sometimes it is necessary to stop a problem from getting worse and to teach your children they cannot behave in such a manner. Withdrawing rewards and privileges can teach your children what they must not do.
2. In many cases, time-out will be your most effective response to stop your children's undesirable behavior. At other times, however, you may find

that withdrawing a reward or privilege is more appropriate or easier for you.
3. Withdrawing rewards and privileges is an effective form of punishment that is more humane than some other methods, particularly spanking.
4. Some children stop misbehavior in response to ignoring, some stop after time-out, and others stop after losing a reward or privilege. The more skills you know, the greater your flexibility. If you try a method that does not work, you can try something different. One time you can use time-out, another time you can take away a reward or privilege. When you know a variety of skills, you can experiment to determine which of them work best for you and your children.

Practicing Withdrawing Rewards and Privileges

Withdraw rewards and privileges during or immediately after the behavior you want to stop. The longer the delay between the problem behavior and the actual withdrawal of the reward, the less effective this method will be. When parents wait before withdrawing a privilege, children often misunderstand which behavior they are being punished for, and they do not stop the particular behavior the parents are after.

Remove rewards and privileges equal to the misbehavior. Parents should be careful not to take away a major privilege for a minor misbehavior. For example, 7-year-old Molly's parents asked her to get ready to go to her grandmother's. Fifteen minutes later, Molly's parents found her still playing with her kitten and still in her play clothes, not ready to go to grandma's or anywhere else. Molly's mother was very angry and without thinking told Molly that because she did not get ready when she was asked, she was not going to be allowed to go to her friend's birthday party the next day! An example of the removal of a more appropriate privilege for the girl's procrastination would have been, "Molly, because you didn't get ready when I asked, you will not be allowed to pick your own clothes to go to grandma's. I want you to wear your yellow dress. Now get ready."

When parents remove a privilege, it's important they do not take it away for too long a period of time. Instead, they should take away something their children really like for a short time. The advantages to short durations of privilege withdrawal include: (a) It's easier for parents to enforce the removal consistently, (b) Children will not learn to get along without the privilege, and, (c) Children have the opportunity to earn back the privilege quickly or work for a new one through desirable behavior. The negative situation caused by the misbehavior and punishment is ended. Short durations of privilege removal emphasize the parents' teaching that a specific behavior cannot be tolerated. Longer durations of privilege withdrawal, on the other hand, appear to emphasize the child's paying for a transgression or a parent's getting even for the child's misbehavior. Parents must be encouraged to view their role in stopping problematic behavior as teacher and guide, not as lord and master of discipline.

Do not take away the same rewards and privileges all the time. If parents do not vary what they withdraw, their children grow accustomed to being without the reward or privilege. In one case we saw Mr. Shockley tell his 10-year-old son, "Because you were over an hour late getting home and you didn't call, you can't ride your bike for another two weeks." Mr. Shockley's son, Louis, had already been without his bike for over two months due to prior misbehaviors. Louis responded, "Dad, I don't care, I haven't ridden my bike in so long, I've forgotten how."

When parents select a reward or privilege to withdraw, they must be sure to choose one that is meaningful to the children. Just as in presenting rewards and privileges, parents must learn their children's likes and dislikes. Sometimes parents make the mistake of believing some things or activities are important without really knowing what their children value. Parents can learn what rewards and privileges are important by simply watching their children's reactions to the removal of the privilege, object, or activity. When children are not affected by their parent's withdrawal of a reward or privilege, the parents must take note and try not to remove it again.

When you tell children they are going to lose a privilege, follow through. When parents threaten but do not follow through, their efforts have little effect. Their children soon learn that their parents do not really mean what they say and that they will not actually be punished for the behavior they were told to stop.

Some children, particularly those who have learned their parents are a soft touch for a teary eye, will cry or plead with their parents not to follow through with their withdrawal of a reward or privilege. If parents are confident they followed the guidelines for skill use, they should stand firm on their reward or privilege withdrawal. If parents give in to their children's cries and pleas and reinstate a reward or privilege, they will teach their children to turn on the waterworks and begging every time they are punished.

Some parents do not want to take away rewards or privileges unless they have given their children warnings first. If parents want to give warnings, they should limit them to one per problem behavior and they should always give them firmly. Stern voice tones alert children to the seriousness of their behavior and the children learn that a punishment follows the tone if they do not stop. If parents find they are giving many warnings, it indicates they are not following through consistently. When parents use a stern voice, only one warning, and follow through when necessary, they usually find that their children need fewer punishments: Their warnings effectively stop problem behavior.

Do not overuse the withdrawal of rewards and privileges. If parents use this punishment frequently, it loses it effectiveness. When some parents find that this skill effectively stops problems, they try to use it for all types of minor annoyances. These parents remove rewards or privileges for short-term gain when they would have been more effective in the long term using ignoring or suggestive praise.

Continue using the positive skills for desirable behavior. If parents find they are frequently taking away rewards and privileges, it may indicate they are not using their positive skills for the good things their children do. When some parents learn about punishment they stop using their positive skills and depend on punishment to try to get their children to behave well. These skills do not work this way. Removing rewards and privileges can stop problems; it does not teach *desirable* behavior. Parents must continue to pay attention to the good things their children do if they want them to continue behaving well. If parents stop using their positive skills for desirable behavior it is likely their children will misbehave to get their parents' attention — even if it's negative attention!

Parents need to know that if they use punishment frequently, there may be some bad side effects. For example, their children may start to avoid them. They try to avoid being punished and the bad feelings they got when they were punished the last time. When parents notice these kinds of changes in their children's behavior, they must review the frequency and severity of punishment they are using and be sure to increase their use of their positive skills.

Since children can get quite upset when they are punished, it's important parents restrict their use of the skill to only serious, dangerous, or intolerable behavior. If parents follow the guidelines given for this skill, they will be effective and their children will have a minimum of upset. Children will be discouraged from performing problematic behavior, and parents will have more opportunities to use their positive skills for the good things their children do.

Key Points to Remember about Withdrawing Rewards and Privileges
1. Withdraw rewards and privileges during or immediately after the behavior you want to stop.
2. Remove rewards and privileges equal to the misbehavior.

3. Do not take away the same rewards and privileges all the time.
4. When you tell children they are going to lose a reward or privilege, follow through.
5. Do not overuse the withdrawal of rewards and privileges.
6. Continue using the positive skills for desirable behavior.

SKILL 7: PHYSICAL PUNISHMENT

We do not recommend or endorse the use of physical punishment (spanking). We do not discuss spanking in the same light as the other skills. In fact, a primary purpose of this skill lesson is to make it clear, particularly to those parents who have used spanking as a primary method of discipline, that the six preceding skills should significantly decrease or eliminate spanking.

It is essential to note that when we use the terms physical punishment or spanking we mean a few *well-controlled* swats on the buttocks. For some parents, such control is not easily obtainable. For these families, physical punishment must be adamantly opposed. Any form of physical contact that you, as a parent trainer, construe as too severe should be considered abuse and you should not tolerate it.

The use of physical punishment is indeed controversial. Many professionals and parents consider spanking to be inhumane, brutal, ineffective, and unnecessary. On the other hand, many popular child-care books and advice columns endorse physical punishment under certain conditions. Surveys indicate that the use of physical punishment by parents is widespread (Sears, Macoby, & Levin, 1957). Regardless of your opinion on the topic, we recommend you review this section and consider the issues that we address. We have developed guidelines for the use of spanking because we have found that whether or not we think parents should use spanking, many do. Our guidelines are for parents' consideration if they decide, against our recommendations, to spank. We hope that by addressing the issue head on, by encouraging parents to use their other skills before considering physical punishment, and by reviewing the negative side effects and potential abuse of spanking, we will encourage parents to try another way. The same surveys, after all, that show parents' widespread use of spanking also show parents do not like to spank — they would like to handle their children's behavior in other, more positive, ways.

Skill description. Physical punishment involves no more than three brief, firm swats of a parent's palm on their child's buttocks.

Rationale for not using physical punishment. Unlike the other skills we cover in our parent training, we can cite no studies that support the use of spanking.

For a complete overview of the research on the effects of physical punishment we refer the reader to Patterson's (1982) impressive review of the literature. In his review he cited a survey by Stark & Envoy (1970) that showed 84% of American parents spanked their children. These data demonstrate there is a need for guidelines for spanking to help those who use it avoid abusing their children. Before we give parents our guidelines for spanking, we present a professionally balanced, albeit personally biased, rationale for parents *not* to use it.

Physical punishment has many negative side effects. We spend much of our time introducing spanking to parents by reviewing some of the serious negative side effects associated with it. One negative result is that everyone involved—parents and children—become emotionally upset. Everyone feels bad.

Another negative by-product of spanking is that, when it is used often, children start to withdraw and fear, and avoid their parents. Rather than risk being spanked, they just stay away from their parents altogether.

When parents spank, they may accidentally teach their children to try to solve problems by aggression or violence. It would not be surprising to find that children whose parents spank often are known as bullies at school. Siblings who fight frequently may be imitating their parents' use of physical force.

When parents rely heavily on physical punishment to control their children when they are young, they will be at a loss when their children get too big to swat. Some parents spank because they can. That is, their children cannot directly retaliate as they would if they were an adult or larger child. Even though this condition of size may allow the parent to use physical punishment when the child is small, when the child gets older, and larger, spanking may no longer be effective. In some families in which spanking has been frequent, when children become adolescents they are routinely disobedient in the form of challenges to their parents' authority. When a child gets older, the amount of force it takes for a spanking to have a punishing effect is much greater than when the youth was a child. This amount of force should not be an acceptable part of any relationship and parents should not consider using it with their children.

Besides all the potential negative side effects, punishment rapidly loses its effectiveness if used too often. This can be particularly problematic, because when some parents find that their physical punishment is not working, they keep trying by hitting their children harder and more times. Increasing the force of the punishment will not make it any more effective — it will only hurt a child more and damage the parent-child relationship further.

Rationale for using physical punishment. After we review our rationales for not using physical punishment, we discuss with parents the reality that even though we strongly discourage it, we know some of them will still consider using it. To help these parents make the decision to spank or not to spank, we review a couple of points that might justify its use.

1. Spanking can be a swift method of immediately stopping a serious or dangerous behavior. Remember, though, that time-out can serve the same purpose.
2. Spanking can bring an intolerable situation to an immediate end. A quick resolution of a terrible situation can help clear the air for the parent and child. With the renewed calm, parents can use praise and attention, rewards and privileges, and suggestive praise for the desirable things their children do. Parents must realize, however, that instead of clearing the air, spanking can instead result in children's negative emotional reactions. These emotions can linger and perhaps interfere with the children's receptivity to their parents' attention.

Practicing Physical Punishment

We have tried to make it quite clear that physical punishment is likely to create more problems than it will solve. It gets everyone involved upset, children may learn to avoid their parents altogether, they may also learn that the best way to handle difficulties is by physical aggression, it does not work when children get older, and it loses its effectiveness and can lead to more severe physical punishment if used too often. Some combination of the other six skills will work better than will spanking to stop problems and teach desirable behavior. To eliminate problems, parents can use suggestive praise, ignoring, time-out, or withdrawing rewards and privileges in combination with praise and attention and rewards and privileges.

Despite our admonitions, explanations, and recommendations, some parents still use physical punishment. To help these parents avoid abusing their children and increase the likelihood of their continued effectiveness with the other skills, we developed a set of guidelines for their use of physical punishment. We never cover these procedures until after we thoroughly discuss all of the material against the use of physical punishment.

Physical punishment should be used for only dangerous or serious behavior. Due to the potential negative side effects of spanking, and because it is so severe a consequence for misbehavior, parents should never use it for any but the most serious behavior. Before using spanking, parents must carefully consider whether the behavior they want to stop is worth the risk of the potential unwanted by-products. Once parents have considered the risks of the negative side effects, they should not employ spanking unless they can do so confidently. If parents are not sure that spanking is the best way to stop a problem, they should use one of the other methods they have learned.

When parents decide that a behavior is serious or dangerous enough to justify physical punishment, they must use it immediately. If parents wait to spank until after a behavior has stopped, their children may not understand what the problem behavior is. If the punishment is too far removed from the misbehavior it will have little if any influence on it. In this same vein, it is important that parents do not designate their spouse as the one who will mete out the punishment later. When a child hears, "Wait till your father gets home!" and then gets a spanking from dad after mom reports the earlier infraction, this makes dad the bad guy. The child may start to avoid the father and the punishment is too far removed from the misbehavior.

Keep spanking brief but firm. Physical punishment should clearly communicate parents' disapproval of the children's misbehavior. This means that a brief firm swat is better than several mild taps. Gentle taps may not indicate to the child the severity of the behavior or the magnitude of the parent's disapproval. When parents try to stop their 3-year-old from sticking a hairpin in the electric socket, the shock of the sharp swat on the buttocks will be effective in curtailing more serious shocks in the future – a gentle tap may not discourage future electric exploration.

Do not threaten, follow through. When parents tell their children ahead of time that if they perform or continue a certain behavior they will spank them, the parents must follow through when the children do not stop. When parents threaten, but do not follow through, their children soon learn that they will not be punished and there is no reason to stop misbehaving. Over time, in these situations, the number of parents' threats increases and so does the frequency of their children's misbehavior. The threats serve as attention for the children and they simply misbehave more to get more attention. Sometimes, empty threats of punishment result in children no longer listening to other things their parents say. The children believe their parents do not really mean what they say.

Once you decide to punish a behavior physically, do it every time it occurs. If parents are not consistent with their use of physical punishment, their children will learn they can take a chance on getting away with the behavior. Since parents must spank each time a selected misbehavior occurs, they have to be careful not to choose very many behaviors to punish or they will be spanking their children all the time!

Spank only with your open hand on the buttocks. Children should only be spanked on the buttocks. They should *never* be slapped in the face, shaken, or hit with objects such as spatulas, rulers, wooden spoons, hairbrushes, or switches. These methods and implements are dangerous and can severely injure children. When parents use their open hand to spank their children, they know just how hard they are hitting and should be better able to control the process.

Never spank your children when you are uncontrollably angry. This is one of the most important points parents must remember about physical punishment. If parents become so angry they feel they are losing control, they should leave the room and avoid hurting their children. They can also send their children to their room to avoid the risk of harm. When parents find they hit their children often or they lose control when using physical punishment, they should contact the State Department of Social Services or Mental Health Association for help. You can help parents by giving them a list of names and phone numbers of the appropriate agencies so they can have easy access to assistance and avoid hurting their children.

Remember to use the other methods, particularly those that increase behavior. Once we specify all the guidelines and explain the negative side effects that can accompany physical punishment, we are surprised any parents use it. In spite of our attempts to discourage them, some still decide to spank. We believe that our greatest success at discouragement comes from success at encouraging the practice of the other skills. The six skills parents know by the time we explain the guidelines for physical punishment should enable them to increase desirable behavior and decrease undesirable behavior sufficiently. Physical punishment should not be necessary, or an inviting alternative.

Key Points to Remember about Physical Punishment
1. Physical punishment has many negative side effects.
2. Physical punishment should be used for only dangerous or serious behavior.
3. Keep the spanking brief but firm.
4. Do not threaten, follow through.
5. Once you decide to punish a behavior physically, do it every time it occurs.
6. Spank only with your open hand on the buttocks.
7. Never spank your children when you are uncontrollably angry.
8. Remember to use the other methods, particularly those that increase behavior.

Chapter 3
Putting It All Together

This chapter explains how to help parents integrate the seven basic skills. This skill integration requires two steps, so we have divided this chapter into two sections. In the first section we teach the eighth and final basic skill: compliance. In the second section we cover recommendations for addressing specifically some common child management problems.

The information we present in compliance is usually sufficient to help parents learn to generalize their skills for a variety of situations. In some cases, however, parents have trouble generalizing, or problems are severe and parents need extra guidance. In either case, they require additional information. In the second section of this chapter, we suggest methods for addressing 14 common child management concerns:

1. Arguing and Backtalking
2. Fighting
3. Temper Tantrums
4. Bedtime
5. Mealtime
6. Annoying Habits
7. Household Chores
8. Bedwetting and Soiling
9. Hygiene and Appearance
10. Good Behavior in Public Places
11. Homework
12. School Problems
13. Home-School Communications
14. Using Allowances

When we give parents the opportunity to learn about handling these problems, most individuals select those topics that are relevant to them. Some parents choose not to learn about any of these problems, other parents work at learning them all. Regardless of a parent's interest in any specific child management problem, all parents learn the final basic skill, compliance.

SKILL 8: COMPLIANCE

This skill shows parents how to combine all the skills to teach one important behavior: compliance. Compliance is a general label that addresses the most common parental concern: getting children to do as their parents ask them. In our experience and in the literature (Forehand & McMahon, 1981, Patterson, 1982), parents' most common complaint is that their children do not stop misbehavior or that they do not behave appropriately when requested to do so. Parents complain, "I just can't get my child to do as I ask him," or "Jill won't listen; I tell her to stop and she just keeps on," or "Bobby is so stubborn. I show him how to set the table and he insists on doing it his own way." These complaints are all examples of children who are not complying.

Parents teach their children compliance by differentially applying the basic skills. When they successfully integrate their skills for compliance, parents gain confidence in their ability to respond effectively to most behavioral challenges their children present. When children increase their compliance, they are more pleasant to be around, their parents look forward to interacting with them, and the parent-child relationship improves.

Skill description. Combining the seven skills to teach compliance involves one of two sets of responses. When children comply, parents respond with praise and attention, rewards and privileges, or suggestive praise. When children do not comply, parents respond with time-out, withdrawal of rewards and privileges, or spanking.

Rationale for compliance. Children demonstrate an unlimited repertoire of desirable and undesirable behavior. When parents have mastered all seven skills, however, they should be prepared to respond to most any behavior their children perform. Compliance problems concern more parents, more often, than any other behavior. Due to its prevalence as a parenting concern, many researchers have given it attention.

For example, Forehand & McMahon (1981) devote an entire book, *Helping the Noncompliant Child,* to the problem. Patterson (1982) devotes an extensive part of his book *Coercive Family Process* to compliance. In both of these books the authors thoroughly review the research related to compliance. We refer the interested reader to these works for further information on the topic.

Parents find the following list of benefits useful to understand why they should combine their skills to teach compliance.

1. Noncompliance is the foundation of most child management problems.
2. Teaching compliance will help establish an important foundation for a child's future appropriate behavior. In fact, one parent training specialist relates that it is essential children learn compliance. Patterson (1982) believes that a child who is consistently disobedient (noncompliant) is serving an "apprenticeship for becoming antisocial" (p.32).

3. Compliance is important to teach, because when your children learn to do as you tell them, you can stop a problem behavior before it gets serious or dangerous by requesting they do so.
4. When you combine all your skills to teach compliance you are well prepared to handle most any challenge your children present.
5. When you teach compliance you must thoughtfully individualize your approach to your children's specific behavior. This helps you learn more about your children's likes and dislikes. You will be more effective and your children will be more responsive to you.
6. When you teach compliance successfully, your children's improved behavior will please you, and your relationships with your children will improve.

Practicing Compliance

After most parent-training sessions, parents ask questions regarding their children's problem behavior. Typically, before the skill session on compliance, when parents ask questions we encourage them to do one of two things. If their questions pertain directly to the skill for that session, or a previously covered skill, we help them determine how to implement the skill. If their questions do not pertain to the present or a previous skill, we recommend they continue to handle the problem to the best of their abilities, utilizing the methods they have used in the past. When we get to this final skill, however, and parents are learning how to combine all the skills to increase compliance, we encourage them to ask questions regarding their individual situations. We can usually explain to parents how their children's problem is basically noncompliance. For example, one parent complained that he could not get his 6-year-old son to go to bed on time. We redefined the problem for the parent as noncompliance. That is, the child was not complying with the request, "get ready for bed." In another example a parent complained, "My two girls are always fighting with each other." We redefined this problem as noncompliance with the instruction, "stop fighting."

When parents learn the relevance of compliance, they are usually enthusiastic about differentially applying all their skills to increase it. In this skill, we not only train parents how to use their skills for compliance systematically, we also teach them how to create conditions that make compliance more likely.

Keep requests specific. When requests are stated specifically, they do not require interpretation; children find compliance easier. For example, "empty the wastebasket in your bedroom" specifies one behavior, "Clean your room," on the other hand, is a general instruction that can include many

Putting It All Together   59

behaviors. A lack of specificity can cause a problem: The child's conception of a clean room may differ greatly from the parent's notion of a tidy room. The parent may consider the room clean only when the bed has a bedspread on it. The child may consider the room clean when the bed is made, but only covered with a blanket. Some examples of specific instructions include, "put your dishes in the sink," "turn off the light," "get ready for bed," "put the garbage outside in the garbage can," "put your toys in the toy box," and "it's time for you to start your homework." The level of instructional complexity parents can use is determined by their children's age and ability to understand language.

Make only one request at a time. This guideline helps parents keep their requests simple. Some parents act as if their children are computers: They try to program them with long strings of instructions and wait for compliance. Ms. Bemis instructed her 9-year-old daughter, Pam, to "take the dishes off the table and pile them in the sink with the largest dishes on the bottom and the smallest on top. Then, wash the dishes and put them in the drainer. When the sink is empty, clean it with cleanser, be sure to use steel wool. When that's finished, use the sponge and wipe off the table, but be sure to rinse the sponge out with clean water before you use it on the table. Then, rinse the sponge out again and this time squeeze all the water out and leave it to dry on the side of the sink. Finally, use the broom in the hall closet to sweep the kitchen floor and put all dust and crumbs in the garbage; use a twist-tie on the garbage bag, and put the bag in the garbage can outside and put a new bag in the kitchen can. When you're done with that, let me know; I'll be next door at Ms. Rogers' house." Of course, the girl was not able to do all these things — she could not remember them all. Pam got as far as piling the dishes in the sink.

We helped the mother reduce her requests to one at a time. Her next request was much better when she instructed her daughter to "wash and dry the dishes that are on the table and put them in the cupboard." We also recommended that Ms. Bemis stay near her daughter, and not go to a neighbor's, to see if the girl needs help, and to watch her to see if she complies.

State requests clearly. When parents mumble, speak softly or quickly, and their children do not comply, parents cannot know if the noncompliance is due to misunderstanding or misbehavior. One father with whom we worked was employed as a bookkeeper. In his job he inventoried the warehouse stock of large companies. In his work it was also necessary that he and his co-workers read aloud the names and quantities of stock items to other bookkeepers who recorded the information in ledgers. He did his job best when he spoke as quickly as possible. Much to the detriment of his relationship with his 10-year-old son, he spoke as rapidly at home as he did at work. Due to his quick speech, his son barely understood half of what he said. Often, when the father made his rapid requests, a terrible situation developed. The man would speak fast, his son would ask him, "what?" or when he was not sure his father was speaking to him, he would ignore the man. In either case, the father was not aware that he was speaking unclearly and would respond, sometimes in a low roar, "Can't you do anything I ask you to?" David, the son, may not have understood why his father roared, but he did understand the tone of his father's voice. He would be hurt because his father yelled at him, and the father was upset that his son was noncompliant. We helped the father slow his speech down at home and he soon found his son usually complied with his requests and was not really as "stubborn" and "lazy" as the father had believed.

Parents can check the clarity of their requests by asking their children for acknowledgments. In some cases, parents can ask for acknowledgments by simply asking if the child heard the request. In other cases, parents may want a more formal acknowledgment and ask the child to repeat a request. In either case, when children acknowledge that they have heard a request, the parents should not make the request again.

State requests only once. When parents repeat requests, they indirectly teach their children that the first requests can be ignored. This unfortunate lesson often results in a constantly worsening cycle: parents' first request, children's noncompliance; parents' second request, perhaps a little louder than the first, children's noncompliance again; parents' third request, even louder than the second, and then possibly the children's third noncompliance. At this point in the cycle parents often yell louder, use physical force, or give up on their requests and label their children lazy, stubborn, rebellious, or hardheaded. When parents are certain their children hear their requests, they should not repeat it.

Parents increase the likelihood of compliance with their first request by making it when their children are not involved in favored or important activities. Parents should initiate requests when their children are not involved in activities that they will mind stopping — for example, during favorite games or television shows. Parents should also refrain from making requests when their children are performing important tasks, such as homework. When parents carefully select the times they make their requests they are helping their children learn to comply.

Allow a few seconds after a request for children to comply. After parents make a clear and specific request, they should give their children enough time to stop their present activity and begin complying. Under most circumstances a reasonable duration to wait is 15 seconds. Ms. Berman got into many arguments with her daughter because she was terribly impatient with her.

The problems would start when the mother made a request and would expect immediate compliance. It was common for the girl to hear, "Sally, take out the garbage," "feed your cat," or "come in here and clean out the litterbox!" Within 2 seconds these instructions were followed by, "I want it done now, young lady!" She would not give Sally a chance to stop her present activity before she would admonish her. We taught Ms. Berman to give her daughter a slow count of at least 10 before assuming the girl was not going to comply. When parents are sure they have given a clear request their child has heard and has had time to respond to, they must be prepared to act with one of the basic skills.

Respond during or immediately after compliance with praise and attention; rewards and privileges; or suggestive praise. When children comply, parents should demonstrate mastery of the positive skills: This is the time all their practice pays off. Those parents who practice consistently from the first skill through the seventh will have the easiest time selecting and delivering positive consequences for their children's compliance. An example of a parent following compliance with a positive skill was demonstrated by Mr. Simon when he requested his 7-year-old daughter, Angie, to "please wash the potatoes so we can cook them for dinner." Angie quickly brought the potatoes to the sink and started to work. Mr. Simon immediately praised her, "Angie, thank you for doing as I asked and washing those potatoes right away. We'll get dinner ready in no time".

Mr. Sharp showed his ability to use rewards and privileges for compliance when he was at the laundromat with his 11-year-old daughter, Lisa. When Lisa was taking the clothes out of the dryer, Mr. Sharp, noticed she was having trouble folding pants on the crease. He instructed his daughter to "hold the cuffs of one leg together at the seam, then do the same with other leg. Now put all the seams together, making sure the legs aren't twisted." Lisa followed his instructions and folded the pants nicely. Mr. Sharp rewarded his daughter's compliance with "Lisa, for following my instructions and doing such a good job on those pants, you can sit down and read your book. I'll finish getting the rest of the clothes ready."

Mrs. Pasternak's 8-year-old son, Ben, often whined and complained when his mother told him it was bedtime. She decided to use suggestive praise when Ben complied with her bedtime instruction. Luckily, the first night the mother wanted to use suggestive praise, Ben complied with her request. Ms. Pasternak instructed Ben to "turn off the television and get to bed." Ben turned off the TV and his mother responded, "Ben, you turned off the television without whining. It's great when you go to bed on time."

Respond to noncompliance with time-out, withdrawal of rewards and privileges, or spanking. When children have had enough time, but have not complied, parents should respond with punishment. Ms. Friedlander asked her 7-year-old son, Matthew, to "Please empty the wastebasket in your room." Matt paid no attention to his mother. A stranger viewing the scene might have thought Matthew was deaf. Ms. Friedlander counted to herself, "one, two, three," and Matt still did not go to his wastebasket. The woman finished her self-count to 10 and then calmly walked to Matthew, took hold of his arm and said, "Matt, I asked you to empty your wastebasket and you didn't; for that you will spend three minutes in time-out." Matt responded, "I didn't hear you!" Ms. Friedlander had been careful to speak clearly and loudly, so she was confident Matt had heard her. She correctly followed the steps in time-out. Matt complained about the unfairness of time-out and his mother ignored him. When she sat Matt in the time-out chair, he was still complaining. Ms. Friedlander let go of his arm, and said, "Your three minutes won't start until you're quiet," and she walked away. Matt soon became silent and waited for the 3 minutes to pass.

After noncompliant children complete their stay in time-out they should be given another chance to comply with the request. If the children comply, the parents should respond with praise and attention, rewards and privileges, or suggestive praise. When Matt finished his time in time-out, his mother told him, "You can leave time-out now. Please empty the wastebasket in your room." This time, Matt complied with his mother's request and emptied the wastebasket. Ms. Friedlander put her arm around Matt and said, "Honey, thanks for emptying the wastebasket. When you help keep your room clean it really makes things nice around here." If Matt had not complied with the second request, his mother would have repeated the steps for time-out.

Parents can remove rewards and privileges when their children are noncompliant. Mr. Chin's daughter, Vanessa, did not follow his instruction to "help clear the table." Instead, the girl called a friend on the telephone. Immediately, Mr. Chin went to his daughter and said, "Vanessa, you cannot use the telephone this evening until you clear the table." Vanessa responded, "But, Dad, I promised I'd call Sheri right after supper; she's going to help me with my math homework. Besides, I cleared the table last night, it's Jimmy's turn." Mr. Chin did not say a word. He knew from previous conversations he had overheard between his daughter and Sheri that the girls were probably going to spend most, if not all, of the time talking about nonacademic topics. Mr. Chin was mad at Vanessa for arguing back; he wanted to scold her. To refrain from scolding, he purposefully ignored Vanessa by counting to himself from 1 to 10. He did not let his daughter's pleas sway him. When his daughter quieted down, he simply repeated, "You can use the telephone after you've cleared the table." Vanessa reluctantly went to the kitchen and cleared the table. When she was almost finished, Mr. Chin used his positive skills for her compliance and gave his daughter praise and a privilege. The father said, "Van, I appreciate your help around here, you do many things that I'm really thankful for. As soon as you put the butter dish in the refrigerator you can call Sheri."

It is important that we discuss spanking as a parental response to noncompliance. *We do not endorse the use of physical punishment.* We know, however, that some parents will use it in spite of our emphasis on the potential negative effects of spanking. We attempt to discourage parents from using spanking for noncompliance by reiterating the possible side effects and explaining that if parents decide to use it, they must reserve it for only the most serious or dangerous behavior. As an example, we have told parents, "If your children run into the street and you call them back, but they do not comply, that may be a time when you decide to use spanking to impress upon them the danger of the street and your absolute intolerance of their getting off the curb." We also point out that time-out can serve the same function as spanking and is preferable. As a final point, we emphasize that when parents practice their skills to teach compliance each day, their children will be as likely to comply with the request, "Wash your hands before you come to the dinner table," as they are with the direction, "Get out of the street". With diligent practice of praise and rewards for compliance; spanking, time-out, and removing rewards and privileges become less necessary.

Start with two requests per day and then increase the number. Parents should start teaching compliance by concentrating on two requests per day and then slowly working up to more. Parents will find it helpful to request behavior that can be performed every day. For example, parents who want their children to keep their room clean can one time request, "please empty your wastebasket," and another time instruct, "hang your clothes in the closet." Additional examples of requests that can be repeated daily include "please walk the dog," "hang the towel up after you dry your hands," "limit your phone call to five minutes," "wash your hands before dinner," "please call your sister in for lunch," "it's time you took your shower," "please turn the stereo down," and "help your little brother get ready for bed." Just about any behavior is appropriate for parents to use, as long as it occurs almost every day.

When parents have mastered giving two requests and following through, they can increase the number. The additional requests must be specific and address things children do every day. Ms. Washington focused on four requests in one day. She asked her 7-year-old daughter, Bliss, to "please come in to dinner," "put on your jacket before you go outside," "play with that ball outside," and "brush your teeth before you go to bed." After each of these requests, Ms. Washington followed through with her basic skills and helped Bliss improve her compliance.

When children comply consistently, make requests more complex. When parents consistently make at least two clear and specific requests each day, master responding appropriately with the basic skills, and their children comply consistently, they can increase the complexity of their requests. Even though requests can be more complex, they must be stated clearly and specifically. An example of Mr. Harding's four simple requests in one day included. "John, bring the dog inside now," "please put your bike in the shed," "put your computer game away," and "John, turn the radio off while you do your homework." Mr. Harding's 12-year-old son was usually compliant with his father's requests, so Mr. Harding made his requests more complex. Some of the new requests included. "John, you sit here behind the wheel of the car and turn the key to the right when I say to. Don't do anything else"; "Son, you hold Spot's leg with your right hand here, by his elbow joint, and your left here on his foot. Once you have his leg held securely, I'll clip his nails"; "John, put the dishes and silverware on the table and then stir the sauce in the pot on the stove until I check it again"; and "On your way home from school today, please stop at the store and pick up a quart of milk. Here's the money for it." Mr. Harding made sure to continue his correct use of praise and attention, rewards and privileges, or suggestive praise each time his son complied. Each time the 12-year-old did not comply, Mr. Harding removed a reward or privilege.

John complied appropriately with most of the new, more complex instructions because Mr. Harding had laid a solid foundation for compliance. The father started with simple instructions and consistently and appropriately responded during his son's compliance and noncompliance. Mr. Harding then increased the number of his instructions each day and, finally, he made his instructions more complex. When he successfully put his skills together for John's compliance, there were some positive benefits. The boy was proud of himself when his father gave him increased responsibility in the family. Mr. Harding was proud of John because he now followed many complex instructions instead of complaining or avoiding work around the house.

For some parents, teaching their children to do as they have been told can be extremely difficult. Parents' effectiveness will be determined, to a large extent, by the amount they practice. You have to help parents select two instructions they can use each day, and then encourage and praise their practice. If parents do not practice every day, they will not have enough opportunities to become proficient at discriminating which of their skills to use. Also, when parents do not practice, their children may not have sufficient occasions to learn compliance.

Consistent practice is additionally important because noncompliant children do not learn compliance in one day. Parents must usually demonstrate a good deal of patience as they teach compliance. Try to help parents have realistic expectations about the degree and speed their children will improve. No children, after all, do everything they have been told all of the time.

Key Points to Remember About Compliance:
1. Keep requests specific.
2. Make only one request at a time.
3. State requests clearly.
4. State requests only once.
5. Allow a few seconds after a request for children to comply.
6. Respond during or immediately after compliance with praise and attention, rewards and privileges, or suggestive praise.
7. Respond to noncompliance with time-out, removal of rewards and privileges, or spanking.
8. Start with two requests per day and then increase the number.
9. When children comply consistently, make requests more complex.

CHILD MANAGEMENT PROBLEMS

In this section we present the key points for addressing 14 child management problems. We developed the list of problems after many hours of discussion and review with our Parents Advisory Council. The list is not exhaustive, of course, but most parents find we have covered their primary concerns. We teach parents the specific child management information by covering the relevant key points and explaining how to integrate and generalize their basic skills.

Arguing and Backtalking
1. When you can, ignore sassy comments and attempts to start arguments.
2. Remember to use suggestive praise when your child does not argue or talk back.
3. Use rewards and privileges and praise and attention for cooperation and courtesy.
4. If your child's arguing or backtalking gets particularly nasty or intolerable, use time-out or remove a reward or privilege.

Fighting
1. Stop serious fights immediately by using time-out.
2. You can also stop fights by removing rewards and privileges.
3. Ignore children's pleas and promises that no more fighting will occur; punish immediately.

4. Ignore arguments about who started a fight. If you did not see how the fight began, punish both fighters equally.
5. If you see a child start a fight, attend to the victim who has been picked on and punish the bully.
6. Physical punishment should only be used for the most serious fighting, and you should be reluctant to use it.
7. If you decide to use physical punishment, be sure to use it according to the guidelines, and do not use it if you are uncontrollably angry.
8. Physical punishment should only be a temporary measure. It does not teach constructive ways to interact, and it models the behavior you want your children to stop.
9. If fights occur frequently over the same things, institute rules that can inhibit the disagreements.
10. When children follow the rules, cooperate, and play well together, use suggestive praise and rewards and privileges.
11. Set a good example for your children. Try to deal calmly with your children and other adults when things upset you.

Temper Tantrums
1. If tantrums have been occurring for a long time or are severe, you must be prepared for hard work. It may get worse before it gets better.
2. Children generally have tantrums because they have learned it gets them what they want.
3. Do not give your children what they are tantrumming over. Instruct them once that they will not get what they are tantrumming over and ignore any complaints.
4. For persistent and intolerable tantrums, you may want to use time-out. If you decide to use it, do it immediately. While you wait, your child may get more out of hand and time-out will be harder to use.
5. Once you use time-out for tantrums, use it every time your children tantrum.
6. You can also remove rewards and privileges to stop tantrums. Ignore complaints.
7. Tantrums are easier to prevent than to stop. Use suggestive praise when your children do not tantrum.
8. You can also use praise and rewards and privileges when your children cooperate and accept "no" for an answer.
9. Never bribe your children to stop a tantrum. Once a tantrum starts, use ignoring, time-out, or remove a reward or privilege.
10. Set an example for your children; do not have tantrums yourself. Show your children you can handle difficult or frustrating situations calmly.

Bedtime
1. Bedtime should be the same time every night. Weekend and weekday nights can be different, but establish a routine and stick to it.
2. Choose bedtimes carefully. Younger children need more sleep than older ones. Regardless of children's age, if they often act tired during the day, they need an earlier bedtime.
3. Once you have set a bedtime, let your children know a half hour early that bedtime is approaching. You can tell the children that bedtime is near and they should get ready, brush their teeth, and put on their pajamas. Use praise and attention when they comply.
4. If children complain about getting ready for bed, put them to bed immediately.
5. A few minutes before bedtime, briefly remind the children that bedtime is close.
6. When bedtime arrives, make one firm request to go to bed.
7. If the children go directly to bed use praise and attention, rewards and privileges, or suggestive praise.
8. If your children complain about bedtime, ignore their complaints. Remove a reward or privilege or use time-out. Ignore any sassing, wisecracks, or whining.
9. If bedtime has been a serious problem you may decide to use physical punishment. We recommend using the other skills you have learned instead. If you do decide to spank, remember to follow the guidelines.
10. If your children fuss after they are in bed, for a glass of water, for example, and you are sure they are fine, ignore their requests.

Mealtime
1. Even though you might be busy, keep mealtime pleasant.
2. Use suggestive praise, rewards and privileges, and praise and attention when children demonstrate good table manners.
3. Set a good example by using correct table manners yourself.
4. You can use mealtime to teach children healthy eating habits by discussing balanced diets and appropriate food choices.
5. You can help children learn to eat healthfully by keeping junk foods out of the house and by stocking up on nutritious snacks, such as fruit and vegetables. Remember to praise your children for eating nutritiously.
6. Help children learn to try new foods by preparing the food attractively and tastefully, by requesting they only taste the food, and praising or rewarding their attempt. You can also set a good example by sampling new food yourself.
7. Your children do not have to like or eat everything. We all have our preferences. As long as you serve a variety of foods and your children eat much of it, they will receive the nutrients they need.

8. Do not teach your children to be overeaters. When they say that have had enough, let them stop. If you force them to finish everything on their plate, you will teach them to ignore how they feel and to eat just because the food is there.
9. If children act up at mealtime, try to ignore the behavior. Use mealtime as an opportunity to communicate with your children.
10. If you cannot ignore acting up at the table, use time-out briefly.

Annoying Habits
1. Crying, nagging, whining, tattling, baby talk, and complaining are annoying habits that can really be aggravating.
2. Ignore annoying habits whenever they occur.
3. Use suggestive praise whenever your children do not perform their annoying behavior.
4. Remember to use praise and attention and rewards and privileges when children are not behaving in their annoying manner.
5. If the habits are so annoying you find them intolerable, use time-out or remove a reward or privilege. You must remember, however, to use the punishment every time your child performs the aggravating behavior.
6. Before you label a behavior an annoyance, be sure it is not appropriate. For example, if children cry after an injury, the crying is appropriate. Or, if they tell you about something someone is doing that is dangerous, that is not annoying tattling.

Household Chores
1. All people who share the same house should share responsibility for its upkeep. Children have no exemption.
2. Chores teach children useful responsibility. They can learn cleaning, cooking, and general maintenance.
3. If children have not been doing chores regularly, it will take some effort to get them to start. It may help to establish a chore chart that shows clearly who is expected to complete what chores on which day. You can also use the chart to specify the time and frequency for chore completion.
4. Start the chore chart with a few simple chores. Add chores and increase their difficulty as your children get better at chore completion.
5. When children complete chores, you should use praise or rewards for their accomplishment.
6. If children do not complete assigned chores, do not nag them. You can remind the child once, but no more. If the chore does not get done, remove a reward or privilege.
7. You can make children's allowance contingent on chore completion. For example, taking out the trash can be worth 25 cents a day, and making the bed can be worth 10 cents a day. If children do not complete their chores, they do not receive their full allowance.

8. If you pay children for their chores and they start to ask for money for all tasks, tell them they will only get paid for tasks when you decide. If they ask again, ignore the nagging.
9. Chores should be shared by everyone in a household; be careful not to overload one child.
10. Do not treat your children like slaves simply because you can get them to complete chores. You will teach them best to do chores by being a good example and by sharing household responsibilities with them.

Bedwetting and Soiling

If your children have a problem learning correct bathroom habits, have them examined by a doctor before you try anything else we recommend. Your doctor will be able to tell you if a medical problem is causing the wetting or soiling.

Bedwetting
1. Bedwetting does not mean your children have an emotional problem. Nearly all children wet their bed; most children stop on their own. You can help them stop.
2. First, do not allow your child to drink any liquids for two hours before bedtime.
3. Be sure your child goes to the bathroom just before bedtime. Use suggestive praise for using the bathroom and trying not to wet the bed. You can also promise a reward in the morning if the bed is dry.
4. If the bed is dry in the morning, give the reward as promised. Be sure to make a big deal out of the dry bed.
5. If the bed is wet do not make a big deal. In a matter-of-fact tone tell the child to wash and get dressed. Do not mention the wet bed or the reward. If your child brings it up, just say, "We'll try again tonight."
6. Follow these steps every night for a week. If the bed is wet less often, keep up the good work! Continue to give rewards and lots of praise.
7. If you do not follow these steps consistently, do not expect a dry bed. Continue these steps for two more weeks, until your child's bed is dry most of the time. Do not worry about an occasional accident and do not discuss it.
8. After two weeks you can stop giving rewards every day. Reduce your rewards to once after every two or three dry days in a row. Explain the changes in the reward schedule to your child.
9. Most children will stop wetting the bed if you follow these steps. If your child does not stop, there are some new steps to add to the ones you have been following. The steps to follow now are:

A. No liquids two hours before bedtime.

B. Send your child to the bathroom before bedtime.

C. Wake your child every hour to use the bathroom until you go to bed.

D. If the bed is dry, use lots of praise. If the bed is wet, have your child wash up and change the sheets.

E. In the morning wake your child 15 minutes early. If the bed is dry, give praise and a reward. If the bed is wet, make your child wash up and change the sheets.

10. Even though these steps are time consuming you must follow them until your children are dry five nights in a row. When you see this progress, you can stop waking them every hour in the evening. Instead, wake them only once, just before you go to bed. Be sure to keep up with the other steps.
11. Keep using rewards until your child is staying dry nearly all the time. A small reward after every two or three dry nights should be enough. Do not stop using rewards too soon or the bedwetting may get worse again.
12. Even when your child stays dry nearly all the time, there may be a slip-up every now and then. When this happens, have the child change the sheets, but do not discuss the accident. Be sure to use praise and a reward the next time the bed is dry.

Soiling or Wetting Clothing
1. Most children have accidents once in a while. Usually, they occur because the children are tired, upset, or they got so involved in an activity, that they forgot to use the bathroom.
2. If the accidents are infrequent, such as once or twice a month, the best thing you can do is ignore them. Do not scold or nag, just have your child wash up and change clothes.
3. If the soiling or wetting clothes happens often, you will have to help your children learn better bathroom habits. You can begin by checking their clothes every half hour. You can usually tell if there has been an accident by sight or odor.
4. If your check shows clean clothes, use lots of praise. Then ask your children if they need to use the bathroom. If they go, use suggestive praise for not having an accident. After three or four clean checks in a row, give your child a small reward or privilege.
5. If your check shows soiled clothing tell your child to wash up, change clothes, and rinse out the soiled clothing. Do not give a lot of attention during clean up. Handle the situation quickly and firmly, and have the child do as much alone as possible.
6. Follow these steps consistently until your child has three days in a row with no accidents. If you are consistent, this should only take a few days.

After three clean days in a row, start checking your child's clothing every hour or two instead of every half hour.
7. Praise for clean clothing, ask your child to use the bathroom. After three or four clean checks, give a reward or privilege. For soiling, have your child clean up, change clothes, and rinse out the soiled clothing. Then, remove a reward or privilege. After a week of clean clothes you can start checking your child's clothes once or twice a day, instead of every two hours.
8. When you find your child's clothing has been clean for another week, you can stop the checks. Remember to occasionally use suggestive praise and rewards and privileges for clean clothes.
9. Even when your child stays clean most of the time, there may still be accidents once in a while. Try to remain calm. Have your child clean up, change clothes, and rinse out soiled clothing. Then remove a reward or privilege. Be sure to use suggestive praise when you see that your child has not soiled or wet.

Hygiene and Appearance
1. One of the most common things parents teach their children is good hygiene habits. These can range from brushing teeth and thorough bathing to changing underwear and selecting clean clothing.
2. When children are young they can learn simple things, such as brushing their teeth. As children get older they can learn more difficult hygiene skills, such as, clipping their nails.
3. Children learn good hygiene more readily when you set up a regular schedule of self-care. For example, a bath every night before bed or combing hair before going to school will help children develop good hygiene as a habit.
4. Be a model of good hygiene to your children.
5. Make good hygiene fun. For example, inexpensive bath toys or bubble bath can make bathing an experience your children look forward to.
6. Use praise and attention, rewards and privileges, and suggestive praise when your children perform good hygiene.
7. Do not repeat instructions to perform hygiene behavior. If your child does not comply with your first request, remove a reward or privilege.
8. When children get older you should increase their responsibility for self-care. You can, for example, allow them to select their clothing as they get dressed each day. You can help them learn to select appropriate clothing by giving them options, of which you approve, and letting them choose.
9. When children can demonstrate they can make responsible choices, you can allow them to help select the clothing you purchase for them. In some cases you may disagree with their selections. If you cannot compromise, you may have to disallow a purchase. If you can, however, learn a little

about current fashions among children your children's age, you may be more sympathetic to their choices and you might find compromising a little easier.
10. As your children grow older there may be special hygiene problems, such as body odor, pimples, and menstruation. Never embarrass your children about these issues, discuss them in a matter-of-fact manner. You can express pride in your child's increasing maturity, and your discussions about personal issues can strengthen your relationship.

Good Behavior in Public Places
1. Going to public places with your children can present special problems. But if you follow some important steps, you can teach your children to be well behaved in public.
2. Start teaching good behavior in public with short trips. Fifteen-minute trips to the grocery store or five-minute trips to a neighbor's home are good beginnings.
3. Before entering the place you are visiting, explain specific rules of the visit. By telling children ahead of time what you expect of them, you set the stage for desirable behavior.
4. You can encourage desirable behavior by telling your children there will be a reward at the end of the trip if they follow the rules. For example, you can tell your child, "If you do not ask for candy or toys during our time in the grocery store, you can pick one kind of candy when we get to the checkout."
5. You can help your children stay out of trouble by involving them during the trip. For example, in the grocery store you can ask them to help select a cereal, and in a visit to someone's home you can ask the child to tell about something that you know happened at school.
6. Use praise, rewards, and suggestive praise for good behavior throughout the trip.
7. Ignore as much minor misbehavior as you can.
8. For inappropriate behavior you cannot tolerate, use time-out or remove a reward or privilege.
9. For extremely serious or dangerous behavior you may decide to use physical punishment. If you do use spanking remember to follow the guidelines and never use it when you are uncontrollably angry.
10. Do not allow your children to use the excuse of being in a public place to stop you from responding to their misbehavior the same way you would if you were at home. For example, using time-out may be difficult and embarrassing, but you can do it effectively. Find a dull corner, or similar place, and have your child stay there for three to five minues. Ignore crying and pleas to leave, just as you would at home. Also, be sure to ignore the looks or reactions of others. Do not bribe your child to stop

misbehaving because you are embarrassed. Be confident that you are making the best parenting decision for your child.
11. Gradually increase the duration and frequency of trips as your child demonstrates good behavior in public places.

School Problems
1. Sometimes children get in trouble at school. Some problems are with classmates, other problems are with teachers. In either case, you might become involved.
2. If you are requested to visit with your children's teacher because of a school problem, there are some important steps you can follow to help your children solve their problems. Let the teacher know you will help.
3. Have the teacher describe the problem completely so you are sure you understand it.
4. Observe in the classroom if you need more information.
5. Ask for suggestions regarding how you can help.
6. If you try what the teacher recommends, but the problem does not improve, return to the teacher and request further recommendations. Try to continue to work in a partnership with the teacher to solve the problem.
7. Incorporate your child management skills at home. Use praise, rewards, and suggestive praise for the desirable behavior, and use time-out or remove rewards for behavior that must stop. If possible and appropriate, ask the teacher to use these skills too. Try to have everyone involved working together for the good of your child.
8. Tell your children that you are working with the teacher. Be sure they know that you and the teacher will be keeping in close contact about the school situation.
9. Be positive about education. Unless you show respect and interest for learning and education, your children are unlikely to care either.
10. If the problem persists, use a home-school report card. We explain the steps to use this card in the section on home-school communications.

Homework
1. Homework is an important part of education, it can directly affect the grades children receive.
2. Even though children need time to play and relax, it is also important that they do homework regularly and get into the routine of reading and sharpening their academic abilities.
3. Show an interest in your child's homework. Use praise and rewards and privileges for a positive effort and work well done.
4. If you have a serious problem getting your children to do their homework, telephone the teacher and discuss the situation.

5. Ask the teacher to explain the kind and amount of homework your child should be doing regularly. You can then be a better judge of the accuracy of your child's claim, "I don't have any homework tonight."
6. Tell your children you discussed their homework problem with their teacher. This is sometimes sufficient to get your children to do their homework on a more regular basis.
7. Let your children know that you expect them to do homework every night. Also, tell them you will help them all you can.
8. When you do help with homework, be a guide. Do not do the homework yourself.
9. Homework should be scheduled regularly, and your children should complete it before they can participate in favorite activities.
10. Set aside a study area where your child will study each day. It can be a kitchen table or desk in a bedroom, but it must be quiet and conducive to concentration.
11. Check over the homework. Review the accuracy and neatness, using praise and rewards for good work. Matter-of-factly tell the child to re-do any work that needs it.
12. Encourage your children to do homework by:
    A. Being positive about education.
    B. Do something academic like while your children do their homework. This can include reading, balancing a checkbook, or writing a letter.
    C. Offer special rewards for improved grades on homework, tests, and report cards.
    D. Do not assign homework types of activities as punishment. Do not, for example, assign writing definitions from the dictionary as a punishment.
13. Keep in close contact with your children's teachers so you can monitor their homework completion and academic progress.
14. If your child has a persistent problem with homework, you can start a home-school report card. We explain the steps to use this card in the section on home-school communications, which is next.

Home-School Communications
1. If your child has had ongoing problems at school and you and the teacher have tried to solve the problems with no success, you may find it helpful to start a home-school report card system.
2. The home-school report card is a convenient way for you and the teacher to communicate regularly about your child's school behavior.
3. No matter what the specific problem is that your child has, the home-school report card should include the following information:
    A. The child's name.

B. A blank for the day's date.

C. A way for the teacher to report how your child did in school that day. For example, a report could say, "Billy Did/Did Not (circle one) finish all his work in school today." All the teacher has to do on this report card is circle the appropriate category to let the parent know whether the child finished his schoolwork.

D. There should also be a blank for the teacher's signature.

4. Report cards can be used for more than one problem at a time. For example, academic performance and getting along with others. Parents can simply add a statement for each problem the teacher is to report.
5. Report cards can also be used by more than one teacher. The card must have places for each teacher to sign.
6. Report cards seem to work the best when parents and teachers develop them together. This teamwork encourages consistent communication.
7. Once the design for the report card is complete, multiple copies must be made. Some teachers have access to copying equipment and will be able to make the copies. Sometimes parents will have to photocopy or use some other means to get copies made.
8. Develop guidelines for using the report card. There should be a set of positive and negative consequences — in relation to the reports on the card — that will happen for your child each day.
9. Explain the report card system to you child. Be sure that you explain that there are positive and negative consequences for the types of reports you get from the teacher.
10. Be sure to praise and reward favorable reports.
11. Special rewards can be given for very positive behavior and for an increased number of days with positive reports.
12. Remove rewards and privileges for negative reports.
13. To help your child avoid "losing" bad reports on the way home from school, explain that you will use more severe punishment for lost report cards than for negative reports.
14. When you punish for negative reports, do not scold or nag. Use a matter-of-fact tone and explain the punishment. If your children plead or whine, ignore it.
15. When your child regularly gets favorable reports, you can cut down the size and frequency of rewards you give. Continue to use praise and attention and suggestive praise.
16. Telephone the teacher and explain that you would like to change to weekly reports. Thank the teacher for being cooperative and helping your child.
17. If you follow through consistently, you should be able to stop using the daily reports in about a month, and you can change to weekly reports. After one month of favorable weekly reports, you can stop the report

cards completely. Be sure to tell your children that you are stopping the report cards because their behavior has been so good.
18. Tell your children you are going to stay in contact with their teacher. Inform the children that if the teacher relates that there are problems again you will restart the report card. Be sure to explain that if you get no bad reports there will be a special reward.
19. Telephone the teacher and explain that you would like to stop the report card system. Make it clear that you will stay in contact to find out how your children are performing.

Using Allowances
1. You already know how to use rewards and privileges to encourage your child's accomplishments. Allowances are a form of rewards.
2. Parents can use allowances in exchange for all sorts of good behavior. Some parents give them to their children for performing household chores, and other parents give them when their children have behaved well and not problematically. In any case, allowances should be earned.
3. In some cases, parents give allowances after their children perform a few different behaviors, such as making their bed, taking out the trash, and washing the dishes. In other situations parents give allowances only after the behavior has been performed regularly for some specified time period, such as walking the dog every day for a week. Parents can also combine these kinds of expectations.
4. When parents want to use allowances as a reward for a few behaviors or for a few days performance of specific behavior, it can be helpful to use a chart. Parents can put stars, Xs, points, or some other notation on the chart to indicate that the child has completed a particular behavior. An advantage of a chart is that the parents will not have to give a reward (money) each time the child performs a behavior. The stars, points, or Xs serve as a bridge between the behavior and the actual reward.
5. Charts show children exactly how much they have earned toward their allowance goal. This can help encourage them to continue their effort.
6. The chart should be in a highly visible place, such as on a refrigerator door. In this kind of location, it is easy for the children to keep track of how they are doing, and the chart can serve as a reminder to perform a behavior.
7. Parents can use charts to keep track of behavior for exchanges of rewards other than allowances. Some parents use stars, points, or Xs in exchange for privileges, such as late bedtimes or favorite television programs. Parents and children should work together to determine how the chart will work and what the rewards and privileges will be.
8. The exchange rate for a behavior's worth should be set at a level that is low enough to be encouraging but not high enough to be discouraging.

Putting It All Together

Parents' knowledge of their children's preferences and abilities will help them set the level and adjust it.

9. Whenever you give a star or a point, remember to use praise and physical affection.
10. Do not nag children to earn their points or stars. If you have to remind them, the system is not working. When this happens, either the rewards are not important to the children, or they are getting their rewards elsewhere. If you are consistent and deny access to rewards and privileges until your children earn them, the chart system will work on its own.
11. You can give points or stars as special rewards when your children do not expect them.
12. Your praise and affection are essential when you give stars, because eventually you want to stop using the chart. The chart is really just a temporary solution to encourage good behavior to happen more often.
13. After your children are routinely doing those tasks on the chart, it is time for you to gradually stop giving points. One way is to simply cut down on how often you give them. Another way is to drop some behaviors from the chart. In either case, be sure to continue giving praise and attention.
14. Once you have eliminated the chart, you should be giving allowances for a few behaviors that your children perform regularly. Be sure to continue to use praise and rewards and privileges when your children behave well.

Chapter 4
Leading A Group

The teaching methods we describe in this chapter work best when used with a group of parents. A group provides more lively discussion, gives parents support and an awareness that they aren't alone in facing the challenge of parenting, and makes for easier use of role-play exercises. Our groups typically run for eight meetings, once per week, each about one-and-a-half hours long. Allow 30 minutes before the meeting to prepare and another hour after the meeting for individual conferences with parents. Of course, not all parents are comfortable in groups, or you may not be providing service to groups. In these cases, with just a few simple adaptations you can still employ the same methods we've outlined.

GETTING READY

Content Sequence

We introduce the basic content outlined in Chapter 2 in this order: Meeting 1: Praise and Attention; Meeting 2: Rewards and Privileges; Meeting 3: Suggestive Praise; Meeting 4: Extinction; Meeting 5: Removing Rewards and Privileges; Meeting 6: Time-out and Physical Punishment; Meeting 7: Compliance; Meeting 8: Special Problems and Maintaining Change. Content is sequenced with the easiest material presented first and with prerequisite skills taught before subsequent skills, so parents experience success quickly and frequently.

Group Composition

One of the first questions you must answer is, "What should my group look like?" We recommend that you not worry about how heterogeneous or homogeneous your group is. We've led groups with parents from various socioeconomic levels, ethnic groups, and educational backgrounds. We've also led groups comprised of parents whose children all attended the same affluent private school. In both extremes, the groups were quite successful. Also, you should feel comfortable including parents whose children are as young as 3 and as old as 12. Whenever possible, try to include both mothers and fathers. Scheduling group meetings during evenings or first thing in the morning increases participation, especially by fathers. Sometimes a personal invitation from you will influence an otherwise reluctant father, and if you can get one dad to say yes, others are more likely to attend.

We have led several groups that have included friends. From time to time we get calls from a parent who has several friends, all parents on her street, who are interested in participating. This arrangement works well as long as you do not let the friends monopolize the conversation or the group. Be sure during your initial interviews to explore with these parents how important it will be for them to discuss candidly the situations they face with their children, as well as their own experiences using the skills covered in the program. If any indicate that it would be uncomfortable with friends present, make other arrangements.

Avoid arranging a group in which most of the members share common backgrounds but a single member or two do not. For example, it is not a good idea to have all upper-income parents with the exception of one or two low income parents, or all college-educated parents with one high school dropout. When one or two members are noticeably different from most of the other members of the group, they may feel uncomfortably isolated. It is likely that they would not benefit as much under these conditions.

Group Size

The size of the group affects the length of the group meetings, the amount of individual attention each parent receives, the amount of time that can be alloted to practice, group cohesion, and group discussion. Optimal group size depends on the format you intend to use. If your format is designed for parents whose children have severe behavior disorders and you plan to spend considerable time practicing skills and discussing in detail how these skills can be used with each parent's child, the optimum group size would be five to seven families. This may be as many as 14 parents, but it is likely that it will be closer to 6 or 8, depending on the number of 2-parent families participating. If, on the other hand, your format is more didactic, with less emphasis on individual role playing and practice, as many as 15 to 20 parents can participate in the same group.

Adding Parents

Parents should not be added to the group after the second meeting. If you receive a new referral after the first meeting, spend a couple of hours with the parent reviewing the material that was covered at the first meeting and have her join the group at the next meeting. However, if the first two meetings have already passed, it is better for the new parent to wait until the next course begins. This is because the new parent often feels less a part of the group than the other parents. By the end of the second meeting the parents in the group know each other, are beginning to feel comfortable with each other, have already learned at least two new skills, and have shared confidences. Adding a new person beyond this point may be disruptive and uncomfortable.

Meeting Arrangements

Meetings should be held in an environment that is conducive to confidentiality, informality, and flexibility. During a typical group meeting you will be presenting specific information, demonstrating a skill, and asking parents to participate in several role-play exercises. This requires that there be sufficient space for parents to be up and around. You should also have a table for your materials, such as this Guidebook and any other paperwork you may be using. Comfortable chairs for the parents and refreshments keep the meeting pleasant. The meeting room should also be free from distractions. You don't want people walking in and out, doors opening and closing, and you don't want to receive phone calls or messages during the meeting. If you allow yourself to be called out during the meetings for anything other than emergencies, parents may begin to feel that you consider the group secondary.

Be certain that parents know exactly where and when the meetings are held. This avoids circumstances in which a parent goes to the effort to attend a meeting only to find that it was held at a different time or in a different building. If you make it a rule to start on time, you will find that parents arrive at the meetings on time. If the group meeting is to start at 3:00 and it starts at 3:00, after one or two meetings the parents will be there by 3:00. If, on the other hand, you schedule the group meeting for 3:00 but you don't start until 3:15 or 3:30, you may be teaching late parents that it is okay to be late, and at the same time you are telling the parents who are punctual that their time is not important. However, with some groups of parents the norm may be to schedule the group meetings for, say, 3:00, knowing that the meeting will not begin for 15 to 30 minutes. If so, use this time to meet with individual parents and to get some informal feedback about how the parents are progressing during the group meetings.

Babysitting

Usually this can be accomplished at a modest fee and it increases the number of parents who can participate in the group. Sometimes our groups have solved this problem themselves when we've presented it at the first meeting. One group formed a babysitting co-op, with each member missing one meeting to take a turn. Members in another group each contributed $10 for a total of $90, which was sufficient to cover a babysitter and a final session party!

Attendance

Prompts can be used to increase parent attendance. They are especially helpful during the first couple of meetings, until parents start to feel comfortable and part of the routine. One good prompt to use is to drop parents a postcard, which they should receive the day before the meeting, reminding them of the meeting time and location. A friendly phone call the evening before also works well. You will find that these prompts increase attendance substantially, and they let you know how many parents to expect at each meeting. Be alert for parents who make excuses: "I don't know if I'll be able to make it tomorrow. I'm having trouble getting my car started." Excuse making is a reliable predictor of parents who are at risk for withdrawing from the program before completion. If you detect excuse making, confront the parent directly: "Mrs. Jones, I'm sorry to hear you're having car problems. I know what a hassle that can be. I've got a '77 Buick that gives me trouble all the time. Is there anything I can do to help? Is there a neighbor who might be able to get you here? I think one of the other group members can give you a lift home. What really concerns me is that sometimes when parents start to miss meetings they lose interest in the group and don't get the full benefit. I'd hate to see that happen with you, Mrs. Jones."

Supplies

You will need name tags, the Guidebook, any data collection forms you intend to use, and refreshments. You might also want to provide parents with pencils or pens.

Plan

Organize, organize, organize. The way to have a successful group is to organize. Have your materials ready, have your name tags printed, have your attendance register at the door, have the chairs arranged in a comfortable semicircle, and have the coffee made. Good group meetings don't just happen; they are arranged.

Early Arrivals

If parents arrive a few minutes early, you'll have an excellent opportunity to begin forming working relationships with them. Casual, friendly conversation is appropriate. Parents may be eager to report how their week went. You can make them feel comfortable and encourage them to share their experiences. However, try to avoid lengthy conversations with one parent that exclude others; otherwise, you risk teaching the parent to use your time individually and not to use the group. If parents do bring up specific questions about their children, encourage them to bring up the same questions during the group meetings. Explain that the chances are quite good that other parents in the group will have similar questions.

STRUCTURE OF GROUP MEETINGS

The format for each group meeting follows the same steps. These steps insure a smooth, effective, satisfying group. The steps to follow are: review practice record; discuss previous week's experience; define and explain new skill, using examples and rationales; demonstrate new skill; role play with parents; provide feedback; conduct mastery check; and assign practice.

Practice Records

Practice records for each of the basic skills are located in Appendix A. You can begin the group meeting by collecting and reviewing the practice records. Remember to collect the practice records every week at the beginning of the meeting. This shows parents how important the practice record is, and it will help increase their recording compliance. When you collect the practice records, review each one individually. If the parent has recorded anything, make at least two positive comments. For example, you might say, "Terrific! you've been practicing!" and "Wow, look at all those descriptive praises!" Then make one statement about the importance of completing the practice record every day. For example, you might say, "This is a great start. If you will complete the practice record every day, you will really get these skills down."

If the parent has recorded nothing, make a general statement of understanding, such as, "It's been a busy week for you," or "Sometimes it's tough to get everything done during the week." Make one statement stressing the importance of keeping track of practice, such as, "The more we remember to practice these skills, the better we will get at them." Finally, tell the parent to keep working on the practice record and that you will take another look at it at the next group meeting.

If the parent indicates that she has misplaced the practice record, make one comment about the importance of practice. A typical statement here might be, "The practice record is really important. It helps us learn the skills and it lets me know how things are going for you at home." Give the parent a fresh practice record and suggest that it be fastened to the refrigerator door. Then ask the parent to complete the record during the week and bring it to the next group meeting.

The most important point for you to keep in mind here is that the more consistent you are in reviewing the practice records each week, the more consistent the parents will be in completing them. No matter what the parent has done, be positive. Use the same principles with your parents that you encourage them to use with their children.

Discuss Previous Week's Experience

Solicit examples from the group members about their use of the skills during the week. Ask every member of the group to describe an example of when they used the skill for the week and to describe how it went. Encourage them to use any notes they may have written on the practice record. For example, you might say, "Mrs. Chan, I noticed on your practice record that you gave Li half a dozen praises on Monday. How about describing a couple of those situations where you praised him and what his reaction was?" Repeat this for every parent even though a parent may not have completed a practice record. After a parent gives an example, praise the example and describe something about it in your praise. For instance, let's say that Mrs. Barrett said, "I praised Margie for making good eye contact when she talked with others." You might say, "O.K., let's take a look at that. Last week you mentioned that one of the most serious concerns you had with Margie was that she was terribly shy. By encouraging her to look directly at people when she talks with them, you're on your way to helping her get over her shyness."

When parents recall an example, encourage them to describe it as specifically as possible. For example, you might say, "Mrs. Chan exactly what did you say to Li?" This allows you to make sure the praises Mrs. Chan is giving are descriptive, age appropriate praises. You can provide feedback accordingly.

Some group members may be reluctant to describe examples. Nevertheless, it's just as important for you to ask them to recall examples as it is to ask the more outgoing group members. Once they have recalled a few examples during a group meeting and have been praised by others, they will begin to feel more comfortable and their participation in the group will increase.

After discussion about the specific skill for the week, allow time for general discussion about the past week. Try to refer to examples from past lessons and examples that parents in the group provide. You might want to ask a question like, "Okay, now that we've covered your practice of the skill for this week, let's talk about how things are going in general. Can any of you tell us about chances you've had during the week to use the skills from earlier lessons?" As you get to know each family, personalize your questions. For instance, ask Mr. Talbert how Wayne responded to his use of time-out. It's also useful to follow-up on comments or suggestions from previous meetings. If during the fourth meeting you suggested that Mrs. Williams try to increase her use of suggestive praise, at the fifth meeting, ask her how it went. This provides you with feedback about parents' problems and progress and lets the parents know you're sincerely interested in helping them. It also keeps parents focused on learning the skills.

Define and Explain New Skill, Using Examples and Rationales

Once the general discussion is done, you're ready to present the skill for that week. Make sure you're familiar with each of the main points to cover about the skill. These are described in Chapter 2. Your parents might also find it helpful to receive a written handout listing the key points to remember about each skill. (See Appendix B.) Say each point at least twice, give an example to illustrate each point, and ask the group if they have any questions. Try to personalize your examples so the members can see how the skills apply to their situations. For example, you might say, "Mrs. Bass, I've been waiting for this lesson for you because you've commented how much Martha enjoys alone time with you. I think alone time with you will be a very effective privilege that you can use to help Martha work on her relationships with her brothers and sisters." Finally, ask each member to describe at least one situation that may come up in the next week in which they might be able to apply the skill.

Included in Chapter 2 are rationales supporting each skill. Review these rationales with parents to help them understand the importance of mastering each new skill and to anticipate the benefits they will gain from correct use of the skills.

Demonstrate New Skill

Once your parents understand the skill, you can demonstrate it for them. Demonstrations serve several functions. First, a picture is worth a thousand words — that is, your demonstration can show your parents, often more clearly than an explanation, exactly how to use the skill. Second, once your parents see you demonstrating the skill, they will be much more willing to participate in role-play exercises later in the training. Finally, demonstrations encourage active rather than passive learning, so your parents will acquire actual changes in their parenting skills, not just changes in the way they talk about parenting. Demonstrate each skill several times, each under a different set of hypothetical circumstances. In your examples, use children of different ages displaying a variety of behaviors. Solicit situations from members in the group. Your demonstrations should also include your comments to help parents focus their attention on critical points. For example, if you were demonstrating descriptive praise, you would make sure your praise was descriptive, then you would say to your parents, "Notice how my praise included a specific description of exactly what I liked." This lets Duke know just what my expectation's are. Sometimes you may also want to use an incorrect example to teach a complicated distinction. For example, one important characteristic of suggestive praise is that it should sound sincere. A good way to teach sincerity is first to demonstrate a praise that sounds sincere, repeat the praise sounding insincere, then conclude with the same praise repeated sincerely. Discuss the differences between the incorrect and the correct examples with your parents.

Role-play Exercises with Parents

Once you've presented the content of the skill, you're ready to begin the role-play exercises. At first, parents may feel uncomfortable during role-play exercises. You can alleviate their discomfort in part by providing them with clear rationales about why role playing is important. Explain that role playing helps them to learn skills quickly and efficiently and it gives you the opportunity to help them with any difficulties they may be having. Parents will also feel more comfortable if you remain as positive and encouraging as you can. Begin a role-play exercise by demonstrating exactly what you want the parents to do. The key word here is demonstrating — not describing, demonstrating! Show the parents what you want them to do. You may even want to model the exact words you'd like them to say. The more you stage the situation for them to be successful, the more comfortable they will feel and the greater will be their interest in participating. In a typical role-play situation, divide the parents into pairs: Ask one to play the role of the child and the second to play the role of the parent. Then, reiterate the precise instructions to the group about what each person is to do. While you work with each pair, ask the other parents in the group to take turns practicing the skill.

Provide Feedback

After you have observed the pair, provide the parent with feedback about the use of the skill. Keep your feedback specific, positive, quantitative and qualitative, and concept based. Specific feedback describes exactly what was correct about the parent's use of the skill. For example, you might say, "Mr. Edge, you said to Norman, 'Norman, you really were responsible this afternoon. I ask you to come right home from school and pack your suitcase. You did that and got the house ready for us to go out of town, too. That really shows me how mature you're getting.' This praise lets Norman know that you appreciate his compliance with your requests and that you're noticing his good judgment. Praise like this means a lot to Norman."

Positive feedback starts with a description of any and all aspects of the parent's performance that warrants attention. Even if the parent failed to be adequately descriptive, the parent at a minimum did say something. Something is an approximation of the response you're after, so be positive about it. You can follow your positive comments with a description of a way for the parent to improve her performance, and end with another positive comment. For example, "Mrs. March, you made excellent eye contact with Debra when you acknowledged her coming home on time. And, you did comment that she had lived up to her part of the bargain by getting in before midnight. Keep working on your voice tone so it doesn't sound sarcastic, and it would be fine for you to touch your daughter on the hand or shoulder when you're praising her. You're getting the hang of descriptive praise!" Quantitative feedback includes a report on how may times the specific skill was used during the exercise. For example, you might report to Ms. Cooper that she used descriptive praise six times, or that she used four descriptive praises and three suggestive praises. Quantitative feedback provides one measure of a parent's proficiency with a skill: More use leads to greater comfort and better results. Qualitative feedback provides additional information about more subtle aspects of skill mastery. A parent may use descriptive praise five times, but three of the five may lack enthusiasm. Qualitative feedback addresses those aspects overlooked by simple frequency counts. Your feedback must address both quantitative and qualitative aspects of the performance.

Concept-based feedback makes continuous references to the concepts being taught. You are teaching eight skills, each representing a specific concept of child management. When you provide feedback, always make it with reference to one or more of the specific concepts you've covered. The more examples your parents see that illustrate a concept, the clearer the concept becomes and the more proficient they will become in using the skill. If you start to teach other concepts, in addition to those covered here, you'll run the risk of not teaching anything well. Your parents will get overloaded with information and poorly equipped with skills.

Do Mastery Check

A mastery check lets you and the parent know whether the parent is able to demonstrate correct use of the skill a specified number of times under a specified set of circumstances. The skills we've described are taught in a systematic order, starting with the easiest skill first, then progressing to the more difficult skills. In addition, prerequisite skills are taught first; for

Table 4.1
Mastery Criteria

Lesson	Criteria
1. Praise and Attention	5 in 5 minutes
2. Rewards and Privileges	2 in 5 minutes
3. Suggestive Praise	5 in 5 minutes
4. Ignoring	0 attention to inappropriate in 5 minutes
5. Time-out	1 no time limit
6. Removing Rewards and Privileges	2 no time limit
7. Physical Punishment (optional)	1 no time limit
8. Compliance	Deliver two instructions; follow one with positive consequences, one with negative consequences No time limit

example, we teach descriptive praise before suggestive praise, because suggestive praise requires the ability to use descriptive praise. Making sure that a parent can demonstrate mastery of a prerequisite skill before moving on to a more difficult skill helps to insure that the parent will be successful at the next more complex skill. If a parent is unable to demonstrate mastery of a skill, you know then that you must provide additional examples, demonstrations and feedback until the parent can be successful. Each parent is given the opportunity to progress at her own rate: She isn't asked to use a new skill until she has mastered prerequisite skills.

You can set your own mastery criteria, depending on how much time you have for training, the complexity of the skills, parents' entry levels of skill proficiency, and your own estimation of what frequency provides a convincing demonstration. Table 4.1 shows sample mastery criteria we use with a group of eight parents, with each group meeting lasting 90 minutes. Parents are given 5 minutes during a role-play exercise to reach the mastery criteria. No feedback or instructions of any kind are provided during the mastery check. After the 5-minute role play, we provide the parents with written and verbal feedback about their attempts. Appendix C includes sample mastery check forms.

Assign Practice

After each parent participates in a mastery check, it's time for you to assign practice. Distribute and review the practice record, ask each parent to describe one situation during the week where she might be able to use the skill, emphasize the importance of practice, and remind parents to bring the completed practice record to the next group meeting.

Closing the Meeting

Now you're ready to close the meeting. Acknowledge any special efforts by particular parents, for example, "Mrs. Freeze, you really warmed up today on those descriptive praises. They sounded so sincere. I'm sure Toasty will love them." Summarize the main points of the lesson with another reminder of the importance of persistence and practice. Thank the parents for attending the group meeting and tell them you are looking forward to seeing them next week. Be sure to state the time, "See you next Tuesday at 8:30. Is there anyone who won't be able to make it?" Also let them know you'll be available after the meeting to discuss any specific questions not brought up in group.

These are the general procedures to follow for all group meetings. However, there are a few additional points to consider during the first meeting and during Meeting 8. These points are discussed in the sections that follow.

Meeting One

To begin the first meeting, reintroduce yourself to members of the group and thank everyone for their interest in participating in the program. Many parents find it helpful for you to review your personal and professional credentials briefly. If you have children of your own, share a personal war story. If you don't have children, tell the group that you've always wanted kids but you have a rare genetic disorder that you cannot in good conscience pass on to another generation. Spend a few minutes reviewing the main points from the initial interview: that the program will involve some hard work on the part of the parents, that you will be asking them to practice new skills each week at the meeting, and that they must practice the skills between meetings as well. Reiterate that if they have been having difficulties with their children for some time they should not expect the difficulties to vanish overnight. Stress regular and prompt attendance, and require that parents let you know the day before if they won't be able to attend a meeting.

Once you have reviewed this information, begin the group by asking each parent to describe a little bit about their family, their children, and any problems they may be having with their children. Start with a parent whom you perceive as outgoing, one who is likely to share with the group, then proceed around the circle. This type of introduction helps parents realize that they aren't the only ones who have difficulties with their children and it starts to form a cohesive group.

Finally, describe the general format for the group meetings. Explain the first thing you'll do each week is review the practice record, then discuss the skill from the previous week. Then there will be time for general discussion followed by introduction of a new skill. The meeting will conclude with role-play exercises, feedback, and opportunities to demonstrate mastery of each skill.

One other point should be mentioned: Make certain all participants understand that group discussion and events are confidential, not to be discussed with anyone outside the group.

Meeting 8

Meeting 8, or the final meeting of the group, provides an opportunity to tie up loose ends, answer any final questions participants may have, practice skills that seem awkward, and discuss the importance of practice to insure skill maintenance. You can also distribute assessment instruments and collect consumer-satisfaction data. We encourage our parents to exchange phone numbers and to keep in touch with one another. We have even sponsored maintenance groups held once every three months for graduates to reconvene. We've had as high as 75% return rate after three months, with parents reporting that the follow-up meetings were helpful as both skill and morale boosters.

YOUR BEHAVIOR

When conducting a parent training group, your behavior contributes immensely to the success or failure of the experience. How you interact with parents in part determines how much they get out of the group, how willing they become to try new skills, how skillful they become, and how they talk about the experience to other parents with similar needs. Constant surveillance of your own behavior can help you to increase your own effectiveness.

Try to involve all group members. Naturally, in any group, some parents will talk more (although maybe say less) than others. It is easy for us to overlook the quiet or reticent parents in favor of those who squeak louder. This not only does a disservice to the quiet parents but also to the talkers, who don't get to learn from others in the group. There is much truth to the saying, "Keep quiet once in a while and listen to others. After all, you already know everything you were going to say!" One way to involve all group members is to ask questions. If a point has been covered in a lesson or brought up in discussion, it is helpful to ask simply, "Mr. Everett, what do you think?" Even though a member's ideas may not agree with yours, or for that matter may even be incorrect, soliciting input makes the parents in the group feel as though they are part of the group, that their ideas are useful, and that they have something to learn and to contribute.

In much the same way that you encourage your parents to praise their children, you must not overlook the value of your praise to parents in the group. The more you praise, the more they feel as though their contributions are important, the more contributions you'll receive, the more they will benefit from the group, and the more successful the experience will be for everyone. Follow the same guidelines using praise as described in Chapter 2. Keep your praises descriptive and sincere, give your praise immediately after the parent comments, and use the types of praise that fit the parents. Simply acknowledging a contribution will be fine for some parents; more effusive praise may be appropriate for others.

Personalizing your attention can help make the group successful as well. Use the names of the parents and their children. It is much more reassuring to Traci's mom if you ask, "How'd Traci do this week?" than if you ask, "How'd your child do this week?" Use of names lets the parents know that you are truly interested in their children.

While it is important to get input from the parents, it is equally important that you keep control of the group. You are the group leader and parents find it frustrating and dissatisfying if you allow one person in the group to monopolize the conversation or the group to meander on subjects not related to the issue at hand. Each meeting has a specific focus. Part of your responsibility is to see that this focus is maintained during the meeting.

In terms of overall demeanor, personal characteristics such as sincerity, empathy, and sense of humor help to keep parents motivated, participating, and interested. There is no substitute for good listening and no excuse for interrupting or rudeness.

ONE STEP AT A TIME

One of the most important points for you to keep in mind both for your own performance and for that of your parents is that skill acquisition works best when taken one step at a time. Each of your parents will master skills at different rates. Each of their children will respond at different rates. Likewise, your capability to help parents interact in more effective ways with their children will progress as you work with more groups of parents. The principles discussed in Chapter 1 — success, successive approximations, sequencing, multiple examples, practice, feedback, mastery, and review — provide you with the conceptual framework to tackle the tasks involved in training skills. The procedures described in this chapter help translate these principles into specific steps to follow to actually equip parents with fundamental parenting skills.

Chapter 5
Solving Service-Delivery Problems

In this chapter we review some of the problems we have encountered in our parent-training efforts. We will try to help you avoid these problems by alerting you to them and advising you of the solutions we have found effective. Many of the problem-solving methods we explain were taught to us by parents.

Throughout our work, parents have helped us devise, implement, and revise our training materials and methods. We had priceless help initially from our Parents Advisory Council and we have had ongoing input from the parents who have participated in our training. All of the parents have in some way contributed to our program in its present form. Our purpose in consistently encouraging and utilizing parental input was to design a parent-training program that meets the needs of an extensive range of individuals from diverse cultural, economic, and educational backgrounds. Even though we have made important headway toward our goal, we continue to hone our service delivery to fit parents' needs.

Even if we were to identify and employ successfully every precaution and eliminate each problem that may detrimentally affect parents' success, we would still fall short of our long-term program goals if we failed to serve parents from hard-to-reach populations. Parents who come from minority, uneducated, multiproblem, or low socioeconomic backgrounds may be less likely to volunteer for or seek out parenting programs. In this chapter, after we discuss problems that can occur in any parent population, we discuss hard-to-reach parents, their specific problems, and what we have done to encourage their involvement in training.

THE PROGRAM IS NOT WORKING: PROBLEMS AND SOLUTIONS

When you are trying your hardest to teach parents new child management techniques, it is frustrating and disappointing when they do not respond positively or they fail to learn the new skills. There is an endless list of reasons why some parents may not be successful or pleased with your efforts. Since it would not be possible or useful to try to cover every situation, we will discuss the problems we have found most often. Even though we may not specifically address a problem you experience in your parent-training groups, you should be able to adapt one or more of our suggestions to fit your situation. In this vein, we would like once again to stress the importance of your personalized use of our procedures. Generally, the more effort you put into adapting our recommendations to fit the parents' needs in your groups, the less service-delivery problems you are likely to have.

Parent-Trainer Problems

Although we hate to admit it, sometimes our clients do not respond well to our efforts because of something we are doing. Our instruction methods or interaction styles can alienate parents or interfere with their optimum performance. To increase the likelihood that your clients are positive about you and your efforts, it is essential that you utilize the same positive skills with parents that you recommend they use with their children. You must use praise, rewards and privileges, and suggestive praise whenever possible to encourage parents' skill practice. For example, Mr. Mueller, one of the parents who worked with us, related he was only able to practice using rewards and privileges on three days in the previous week. We responded to this information with praise first, "Its great that you practiced three days last week!" Our praise was positive, optimistic, and sincere. We could have said, "you really should have practiced every day," but this might have only discouraged Mr. Mueller from trying at all.

A beneficial side effect can result from praising and rewarding parents for their efforts. Whenever you use these skills, you are encouraging parents to try them. You are modeling the exact behavior you want them to perform. Through your modeling you may help parents learn to individualize their skills, vary the ways they use them, and apply them in a variety of situations.

Even though you try to be positive and encouraging to parents, there may be some individuals who still do not follow your instructions or recommendations. Regardless of the reasons they do not comply or follow through, you must avoid assuming the worst about their interest in good parenting. We have not yet encountered any parents who do not want to learn better child management skills, improve their relationships with their children, and help their children be happier. We rely on this positive image of parents when there are problems. We investigate each situation to learn if there is something we are doing to cause the problem, or if we can do something to help a parent ameliorate a problematic situation that interferes with their training.

Parent Problems

Even though clients pass through the initial interview screening and seem appropriate for participation, there may still be difficulties that interfere with their success. It is important you curb these problems as quickly as possible because some parents' problems will interfere with other parents' performance. This section includes recommendations for handling many of the problems we have encountered.

Tardiness. When parents are late for meetings, they can aggravate all the other individuals who arrived on time and who must waste time waiting for the tardy one. Late parents can cause the end of a meeting to be delayed, which can cause problems for those parents who have other responsibilities to attend to. Starting meetings late can force some parents to leave before a session is complete: They might miss some important information. There are some basic procedures you can follow to prevent and stop tardiness.

The first intervention you try should be aimed at any parent who is consistently late. What is the problem? Is there a scheduling problem? Has the parent started working two jobs, double shifts, or a different shift? Are there new problems at home that cause a parent's tardiness? You may be able to help parents solve their problem and help them get to the group meetings on time. You may, on the other hand, find you cannot do anything to solve the punctuality problem and you might have to encourage a parent to leave the group. You can recommend that this parent participate at another time, when other responsibilites will not interfere.

Regardless of the many reasons parents may have for tardiness, your structure and consistency running group meetings can prevent one parent's tardiness from affecting other's participation. Your consistent structuring will help establish group norms. Once norms are established, individuals who do not fit will be apparent. You can intervene quickly and prevent problems from becoming serious.

One of the most effective techniques to encourage parents' punctuality is to start meetings on time. You should arrive at the meeting site early, make sure all is ready, and be prepared to start precisely at the specified time. When you are early you can praise parents as they arrive: This can encourage their continued punctuality.

When you start meetings on time, it is important you do not restart each time a tardy parent arrives. Parents who are late will have to make up for any information they missed. When you begin the meeting, be sure to praise the group for being on time and encourage their continued punctuality. At the end of each meeting remind participants that many group members have full schedules and depend on each other for keeping up with their time commitments: Reiterate the importance of punctuality for the next meeting.

Nonattendance. Nonattendance can be the result of situations unrelated to your meetings, such as a parents' interpersonal problems. Other attendance problems may be directly related to programming problems, such as meeting times, which you might be able to change. The problem of nonattendance should first be addressed through preventive efforts. Explain the importance of consistent attendance during initial interviews. Parents should know they will benefit most when they attend each meeting. The skills parents learn build sequentially; each one depends on the one preceding it. They cannot progress, therefore, until they make up any information they miss through their absence. You should be sure to repeat this important point in your first group meeting. Emphasize that a new skill will be presented each week: Those who are absent will miss the information, group discussion, review, and practice that are necessary for skill acquisition and mastery.

You can also encourage attendance by making parents feel comfortable participating in group meetings. Praise them when they ask relevant questions, bring up problems they are having with skill application, and encourage other parents. When you praise parents for their offerings, you are letting them know they are important members of the group: They have reasons to believe their participation is valuable for themselves and others, and they will try harder to be active group members.

In some cases, we have found attendance can be improved by telephoning parents. It makes them feel important. We do not call them every week; it is not necessary. Two or three telephone calls between the first few meetings is usually sufficient to prompt regular attendance for all the sessions. You can make the call or a receptionist can do it. All that is necessary is for some contact to be made to let the parent know the meeting is scheduled.

When parents consistently miss meetings you will need to investigate the situation to find if there is anything you can do to help improve attendance, or if some other arrangements need to be made. When parents are experiencing home-based problems that are likely to continue interfering with parent training, you can attempt to help them resolve the problems or you can refer them to an appropriate resource for assistance. Regardless of your approach to their problem, if they do not begin to attend meetings regularly, you should help them make other arrangements. You can help them change their meeting time to a more convenient situation, you might even schedule individual sessions, or the parent can postpone participation until their consistent attendance is possible. In any case, consistent attendance is essential for skill acquisition. When parents attend meetings intermittently, they acquire only partial information and they will not learn that the skills comprise a global approach to child management. They may, consequently, view the skills as simply gimmicks or quick fixes for their child management problems.

Problem Parent Behavior in Meetings

Even though you develop a group of regularly attending, punctual parents, you must be prepared for other problems that can detrimentally affect the flow of a meeting. The most common problems include interruptions, monopolizers, excuse makers, and braggarts. You can try to solve in-meeting behavior problems through discussion with the people who cause them. If an individualized approach does not work, you can then try generalized or group approaches to curb a parent's negative effect on the group.

Interruptions. A frequent in-meeting problem you may encounter is parent interruptions. This is most likely to happen when you say something that strikes a familiar chord and parents are reminded of a situation that they have experienced. They may comment out loud or lean over and engage another parent in discussion. This distracts other group members and diminishes the amount of attention they can pay to your information. You can discourage parents' interruptions by mentioning at the beginning of your presentation that there will be lots of time for discussion when you have finished. If a parent interrupts with a question anyway, answer with, "That's a good question. Let's discuss it as soon as I'm finished covering this topic." There are, of course, questions that are germane to the point and helpful to the group. You would not treat these as interruptions, but rather as part of the instruction, and you would respond to them immediately.

Monopolizers. Occasionally you may find a parent who monopolizes sessions. Your attempts to increase members' participation can sometimes inadvertently encourage monopolizers. For example, if many group members are quiet, but there is one person who is not reluctant to speak, this person consequently gets your attention. The attention may be sufficient to encourage that parent to comment on every issue that arises, which, consequently, inhibits the other group members from speaking.

There is an unlimited list of reasons that may explain someone's monopolizing. Some common reasons might be: anxiety, avoidance of other topics, control, and boredom. Regardless of the specific reason for the problem, if an individualized discussion with the monopolizer does not resolve it, you must focus your efforts on controlling the parent's monopolizing during the meeting.

You can try to control monopolizers' in-group behavior by naming parents and asking specifically for their input. For example, "Tell us, Ms. Jackson, what did Tony do when you gave him his first reward for emptying the wastebasket in his room?" This tactic disqualifies the monopolizer from possible participation. A related technique requires that when a monopolizer raises an issue, you limit the input and then ask other parents for their relevant opinions or experiences. In this way, you turn the monopolizer into a catalyst, instead of an inhibitor, for others' participation.

You must diligently encourage all parents to participate in meetings. This discourages monopolizers. Parents' combined experiences, questions, and comments will multiply your effectiveness and the utility of the training. When parents discuss their situations and attempts at skill application, they will often inadvertently speak to the problems and concerns of other parents. When you respond to and guide a parent through a performance problem, you will likely help other parents solve skill problems they are having. The more problem areas and issues of skill application you discuss, the greater the chances that parents will be able to understand, generalize, and attempt a skill in their own situations. By encouraging and supporting optimum group participation you greatly restrict any monopolizer's development.

Monopolizers can be a problem because they are overbearing in their involvement in meetings. There are other parents, however, who are problematic because they are reluctant to participate in meetings. These parents often make excuses why they cannot use, or why they have not been successful with, the skills you are teaching.

Excuse-makers. Excuse-making parents seem to come to meetings prepared not to like what you say and to renounce the utility of the skills you present. These parents often base their excuses on their previous attempts with skills that seem similar to the ones you are teaching. Some parents renounce skill content as not applying to them. A typical lead-in to this type of excuse is, "I tried that, but. . . ." Regardless of the basis for their excuse making, you must determine if the parent is trying and failing, or just not trying at all. Once you identify the source of the excuse you must help resolve the problems and stop them as quickly as possible. If other parents in the group frequently hear the skills are not working, they might get discouraged. Other parents may learn that they can avoid practice by simply making excuses. A negative, excuse-making group member can sour the meetings for all the parents.

Your individual discussion with an excuse-maker should help you determine whether they have tried the skills and their excuses have some validity, or whether they are only trying to avoid skill practice. When you find a parent has tried a skill, or has a valid reason not to, it may be necessary to try to help that parent work out the problem in order to master the skill. If, on the other hand, there does not appear to be a sound reason for excuses, you should make it clear to the parent that mastery of each skill is possible in only a sequential manner. If parents do not attempt to master all the skills, they will not receive much benefit from parent training: Perhaps they should reconsider their participation.

If a parent's excuses distract other group members, it will be necessary to review the excuse publicly. You must show the excuse-maker's reticence has no relevance to others' skill acquisition, and you must also make it clear that excuses are no substitute for hard work toward skill mastery.

On the other hand, when a parent gives an excuse that is valid, such as, "I can't try to use praise when Jimmy's father's around. He always belittles my efforts and makes me feel two feet tall in front of Jimmy." This can be a valuable point to discuss with the group. In this example, you could discuss generally the importance of support that parents may not be receiving from others. You can make alternative suggestions, such as, "If you find yourself pressed for time because Jimmy's father interferes with your practice, you should deliberately set aside play times with Jimmy — when his father's not around — that will give you ample opportunity to practice your praise." You can also ask other group members for suggestions.

Braggarts. Whereas some parents make excuses for not trying new skills, other parents frequently pat themselves on the back for their efforts and their success. These people may be disruptive generally, because of their obnoxious behavior. They can be particulary harmful, however, if they increase the frustration or discomfort of those parents who may be trying hard but not having much success. In either case, it is important that you stop bragging when it occurs.

In the first few instances of bragging you can simply acknowledge the braggart's claims and immediately redirect the group's attention to another issue. Be careful, though, in this redirection, that you do not select a problem someone else is having. The contrast between the braggart's claim and the other parent's problem may make the problem seem more severe than it really is.

Parent-trainers can sometimes accidentally create braggarts. You may not be using sufficient praise and attention to make bragging unnecessary. When parents are working hard to learn new skills they need your pats on the back to know they are doing a good job. If they do not get sufficient acknowledgment from you, they may start to give it to themselves.

You can also handle braggarts by discussing their behavior with them individually. You may decide to appeal for their help in keeping the group cohesive. You can explain, for example, that "some parents in the group are having difficulty mastering the skills. When you frequently report successes it makes these parents very disappointed; they question their abilities." At this point some braggarts will offer their assistance in bringing the other parents along. Do not let this happen! Explain that the other parents would be embarrassed if someone thought they were having trouble. Encourage braggarts to tone down their self-appraisals and talk to you about them after the meetings.

Parents' Performance Problems

Some parents' annoying group-meeting behavior causes serious difficulties for others. For the most part, however, social interaction problems during meetings will be relatively minor. Parent problems with skill mastery, however, may require much extra effort from you.

Difficulty in Skill Mastery. Parents can get very frustrated and upset when they put forth effort, but have little if anything to show for their work. Many of those who participate in parent training have had many failures trying to improve their children's behavior and they have bad feelings about their child management skills and their children. It is your job to help them avoid another failure.

When a parent is failing to learn a skill, the first thing to do is assess the frequency and quality of their skill practice. If parents do not practice, they will surely have skill-mastery problems. When you find parents are not practicing, you must help them develop strategies for regular practice. For example, we helped Ms. Endler develop a plan to practice suggestive praise on Monday, Wednesday, and Friday between 4:30 and 7:00, on Tuesday and Thursday between 6:00 and 8:00 and on Saturday and Sunday between 10:00 and 2:00. This plan took into account Ms. Endler's involvement in a part-time job and her volunteer work. She specified practice times in which she was confident that she and her daughter were typically at home together and her daughter was likely to perform some behavior appropriate for suggestive praise.

In some cases, you will find parents are working hard and practicing consistently, but still failing to learn a skill. These parents need additional instruction and basic remediation. When parents require remediation you must work with them individually. The first remedial steps require more skill demonstrations and more parent role plays. Vary your demonstrations and parents' role plays to give them many different examples. The more kinds of examples parents have, the better able they will be to generalize to their children's behavior at home. Parents should perform enough role plays so that you are confident they can perform the skill in varied situations. A good rule of thumb for "enough" demonstrations and role plays, to consider the parents have a solid grasp of a skill, is to aim for five of each, with at least two virtually flawless role plays. After two flawless performances you can expect parents to be able to perform the skill successfully at home with their children.

Even after remediation, unfortunately, some parents still have great difficulty practicing a skill with their own children. If you are confident the parents have at least made some attempts to practice the skill at home, but have failed, they need further remediation. The next step involves their children. You can have the parents bring their children to the training site, or you can go to their home, or both. You will have to determine the most useful and appropriate method based on money and time available for these efforts. When you work with the parents and their children you should follow the same procedures you used when you role played with the parents in their previous remediation attempts.

There is, however, one procedure you must add to previous methods when you incorporate children into the remediation. Spend some time getting to know the children. Make them feel comfortable and explain they are going to be involved in "play acting." You should tell the children that their parents are going to be saying and doing things that seem a little unusual, but that you are their parents' teacher and you are going to have them practice some new behavior. Tell the children the play acting is only going to last a short time and you would appreciate their help by following directions and playing along. This situation is sometimes more difficult with young children or when you remediate skills such as time-out or removing rewards. Some young children do not understand "play acting" and when their parents tell them "sit in this chair for two minutes," the children react as if they are actually being punished. When you suspect this may cause a problem, you can try to make as much a game out of the situation as possible. If the situation continues to be difficult, you will have to stop and try another method — perhaps more role play. In these cases, if children get terribly upset, explain to the parents that even though the child would not comply, they likely benefitted from the experience because they learned about time-out or removal of rewards.

In remediation, when parents can practice with their children, you should use the same rule of thumb for assessing their skill acquisition that you did in previous remedial role plays. When parents can demonstrate two flawless skill performances, they are ready to practice the skill on their own. Be sure to keep in close contact with parents who have needed remediation. They may have questions you can help them with, and you may be able to stop additional problems by answering these questions immediately.

One way you can generally help all parents avoid the need for remediation is to encourage and praise their practice. It is important that you pay close attention to their role plays during group meetings to be sure they are grasping and attempting a skill correctly before they try to practice at home. During each session, be sure to reiterate the importance of skill practice, and encourage and praise parents' keeping records of their practice attempts.

Refusing to learn a skill. The parents we have been describing have difficulty mastering skills even though they put forth the effort to try to learn them. We typically help these parents through individual attention and remediation sessions. Other parents, however, those who refuse to learn skills, require a different set of responses to help them stay involved in parent training and achieve skill mastery.

When a parent refuses to learn a skill, it is important you avoid defensiveness. Do not start giving reluctant parents a long string of rationales why they should learn the skill. Your first response should include supportive statements and acknowledgment that they do not have to learn anything they do not want to. Your support helps parents know you are not their adversary, but someone who is trying to help them with their concerns regarding child management. Your consistent support will most effectively help parents learn new skills. If you are defensive or argumentative you will simply set up power struggles between you and the parents. This will be destructive and get in the parents' way of learning. Your defensiveness may inadvertently cause parents to band together against you and your "authoritarian" ways. You will inhibit parents' learning.

Remain calm. Even though some parents who refuse to learn a skill may sound belligerent, it may help you to assume they are not upset with you, but may, instead, be uneasy with the skill you are teaching. Some parents may be uncomfortable due to the problems they foresee trying to use the skill with their own children at home. Parents who think they will have trouble using a particular technique, or think they are not likely to use it, will be reluctant to put their time and effort into listening to you and trying to master the skill. You will have to use your best interpersonal skills to convince parents the skills are sequential and based on each other: They need to master each one in order to master any of them. Only those who successfully learn all the skills will successfully learn the final skill, compliance. It can sometimes help to reason with parents who believe they will not need a specific skill. We explain that they cannot predict the future, and there may be a time when the technique they are avoiding is precisely the response they will need to resolve a presently unforeseen child management problem.

If the previous recommendations do not work, there is one more approach you can try with a particular group of parents, those who have been referred or mandated to your parent training service. This method is only a last resort and should not be relied upon as a sole effort. Reliance on any sort of coercive methods can alienate parents from you and undermine all you are trying to do. You can inform refusing parents that since all skills are cumulative, you cannot adequately assess their skill mastery of any future techniques you will teach. You can further explain that the ramification of their refusal is that you cannot report to their referring agency that they have completed their training. In most cases, the referring agency will have jurisdiction over whether the parents will regain custody of their children. This heavy-handed approach may help you convince a refusing parent to learn a skill, but it is not likely to win you any friends. Although this recommendation may be harsh, if it is the truth, you should let parents know the potential negative results of their recalcitrance.

Refusing to role play. Another kind of parents' refusal may cause you serious problems during group meetings and interfere with your ability to evaluate an individual's skill mastery. Parents who refuse to participate in role plays can annoy other parents, particularly those who are cooperative. You will stall your session too long if you spend more than a few minutes trying to deal with an individual's role-play reluctance.

Parents' reluctance to role play may be more common when the group first starts, but persistent refusal to role play must be stopped before it interferes with others' performance or with the refusing parents' mastery. In the first group meeting it is important to model role playing, explain and stress its necessity in skill mastery, and, if appropriate, have parents role play innocuous situations that can help decrease their fears regarding role play.

You may sometimes find that particularly resistant parents will be willing to role play individually in front of you, but not in front of other parents. If we have been unsuccessful getting the parent to role play in the group and individualized demonstrations are the only way we can assess a parent's skill development, we will allow private role plays. A benefit of these solo efforts has been that some parents have increased their confidence and then began to role play in front of other parents. When we practice with a single parent, we have the remaining parents practice with each other: Everyone still benefits.

If you have tried a variety of methods to encourage and support parents' role play but they continue to adamantly refuse to perform, you should explain that if you cannot view their attempt at skill performance, there will be no way you can claim they have achieved skill mastery, and you will not be able or willing to certify they successfully completed training. This coercive approach may alienate some parents, but if it is the only way you can comfortably assess parents' skill development, it may be necessary.

If your "strong encouragement" does not work and parents still refuse to role play, and you do not need to assess a parents' skill mastery for an outside referral source (e.g., court or child welfare), you can decide on an individual basis how important role play is and whether or not you will insist that all parents demonstrate skill mastery. If you decide role play is unnecessary and you are simply trying to present information to parents, there will be little problem with parents' refusals. If, on the other hand, you believe that role play is essential for your parent-training goals, for an individual or for the group, you may have to dismiss parents who refuse to participate. We have rarely found it necessary to dismiss a parent, but we cannot allow one parent's lack of participation to affect the others' performance, or compromise our standards when assessing skill mastery.

Parent mismatch. Whether parents refuse to participate or they are unable to perform due to interpersonal or other problems, they may interfere with others' success and you will have to reconsider their appropriateness for the group. Some parents seem inappropriate simply because they do not fit in with the other members. They may have peculiar interaction styles, they might frequently stray from the topic of parenting to idiosyncratic or esoteric issues, or they may be belligerent and difficult to involve in group activities. Regardless of the specific reason for an individual's inappropriateness for the group, you must tactfully terminate their participation. You can offer them individual training or membership in another group, but they should not be allowed to interfere with others' performance, or to continue in a situation that is less than optimum for them.

Severe child management problems. Some parents cannot do well in parent training because their children have more severe behavior problems than they can address. The children need professional attention or even placement in a residential treatment center. When we discover this is the case, we work closely with the parents and agencies that we think might be appropriate for the children.

When children get involved with another professional agency we try to cooperate with them. As long as parents have access to their children, so they can practice their skills as they learn them, we encourage parents to continue in training. If parents cannot see their children often, we encourage them to stay in touch with us so they can restart training when they can be with their child regularly.

Avoiding parents' failures. One of the best ways to help parents avoid major problems derives from a thorough initial interview. In an initial interview many idiosyncrasies, unusual communication styles, belligerence, severe child behavior problems, and parents' interpersonal problems can be uncovered. In the initial interview you may decide that an individual may not be appropriate for a particular group, or you might find an individual's circumstances warrant one-to-one intervention rather than a parent-training group. In any case, your initial intervention can help parents avoid an unpleasant and unsuccessful situation.

DROPOUTS

We try to ameliorate problems and resolve conflicts as quickly as possible to curb parents' dropping out. In some parent training, dropout rates have reached as high as 50% (Chilman, 1975). Our dropout rate has been a low 19% through the fourth skill, ignoring. Once parents master this skill, the dropout rate decreases to only 1%. It seems that ignoring may be the most difficult skill for parents to master. In reward for its difficulty, however, when parents successfully learn to ignore, they usually experience marked improvements in their children's behavior.

Regardless of the difficulty parents may have learning the skills, or in spite of the successes they may experience using the skills, some parents drop out for reasons unrelated to parent training. Through postprogram evaluation questionnaires, we have found that parents who discontinued prior to the final lesson have explained their dropping out with a variety of responses. Some of the non-program-related reasons have ranged from "My dog ran away" to "I could only bowl on Thursday night." There may always be parents who lose interest or prefer other activities to parent training, but there are a few preventive measures you can employ to keep down the number of dropouts.

The initial interview can be one of the best measures to reduce the number of dropouts. We are not recommending stringent initial interviews for the purpose of screening out "undesirable" parents in order to improve success statistics. We are, however, recommending you structure the initial interview to help parents avoid failure, enhance success, and get involved in the service that most appropriately fits their needs.

Some researchers have determined specific characteristics that can interfere with parents' success in training. Your initial interview efforts should be aimed at uncovering these characteristics and then referring those parents who may not be appropriate for parent training to other more appropriate services. Participation in parent training can be a goal for these parents. The characteristics researchers most often cite as potentially interfering with parents' success in parent training include: depression, the inability to classify problem severity accurately, low social class, and limited social involvement (Wahler & Dumas 1984). Blechman (1984) found that when parents' general competence is low, they may need to improve their general living skills, such as self control or marital problem solving, before they can effectively learn and implement new child management techniques.

Bernal (1984) stresses the importance of consumers' knowing what different kinds of parent-training programs exist. In your initial interview you can inform parents of the other parent-training programs available in your area. Thus educated, some parents may select to be involved in a different parent-training program than yours because it addresses some specific aspect of parenting your program does not cover, or they may want a specific sort of emphasis in their training e.g., psychodynamic instead of behavioral. In any case, educating consumers in their initial interviews can help you assess their appropriateness for your parent-training program.

Once you complete thorough initial interviews and have identified those parents who are likely to benefit from participation in your program, there are many things you can do to encourage participation and discourage dropping out. First, and most often repeated throughout this book, give frequent positive feedback and praise parents' efforts often. Avoid negative criticism at all times.

In spite of our attempts to use positive feedback and avoid negative interaction, some parents drop out simply because they do not like our group leadership or interaction styles. We try, of course, to never alienate parents or let our personalities interfere with parents' success. Through our experience and feedback from parents, we have tried to build supportive and encouraging environments for parents' skill development. We have found it important to be responsive to parent feedback and modify our methods to meet expressed needs and desires. Typically, conflicts of scheduling, problem severity and duration, and previous assistance in child management seem to be directly related to parents' frequency of problems in our parent training. If we have selected parents with these problems after their initial interviews, we do our best to help them individually to adjust to our program efforts.

Finally, we have also found that parents' involvement with other agencies or practitioners can stand in the way of their success. We consistently do our utmost to contact any other helping professionals with whom parents may be involved. In our contacts we explain what our program does, how it is organized, and we try to discuss how our efforts can fit with the efforts of the other professionals. Our demonstration of respect, sharing, and mutual effort usually serves to help other professionals support our program with our clients. We have also found out important information from these other professionals regarding parents. This information has often improved our ability at helping parents work with us and benefit from our training. In a few instances we have postponed parents' involvement in our program due to another professional's opinion regarding the client's ability to participate. In these cases, participation in our parent-training program became a treatment goal, for the client.

HARD-TO-REACH PARENTS

We never intend our initial interview to serve primarily as an exclusionary process that keeps "undesirables" away from us. Quite the contrary. We have worked diligently to develop and implement procedures that contact and involve parents who are typically referred to as "hard-to-reach" and unlikely candidates for parent training. We have used these procedures with a variety of parent populations, including: multiproblem families, teenagers, adolescents in populations at risk of becoming pregnant, public aid recipients, and child-welfare clients.

We have implemented a few different methods for increasing our contact of hard-to-reach parents. In one effort we enlisted the help of the local schools to announce we were offering a parent-training program. By a lucky coincidence, teachers sent our announcements home with their pupils' report cards. We received 300 telephone calls from interested parents in the next two days.

In a separate outreach attempt we tried to increase our contact with parents in a low-income, inner-city housing project. Our first attempt was a dismal failure. We offered coffee and donuts to parents who would come to a meeting to learn about our program. Only two people showed up. We next enlisted the aid of the tenants' representative in the housing project and we had great success. The woman we contacted knew everyone, and everyone seemed to like her. Once she showed support, parents got interested in working with us.

After we got the housing-project parents involved in our training, we learned a few important things about keeping them attending regularly. First, we offered them incentives. For each aspect of their participation, parents could earn points. These points were put in a deposit book for them and they could select gifts, mostly toys for their children, in exchange for the points they earned.

We were suspicious that even though we had support from the residents, and parents could earn prizes for participation, there were other problems we needed to address to maintain the involvement of this hard-to-reach population. We offered our meetings at convenient times, on-site at the housing project. Most of the parents were busy and few of them had access to automobiles; if we had not offered training on-site very few parents would have been able to attend. We also anticipated that problems might arise if parents had child care needs when they were to attend a meeting. We did not have enough staff to offer child care, and we believe that would have been an effective measure, but we did handle the problem in another way. We helped participating parents share babysitting tasks so one group of parents could attend meetings while another group performed child care. The parents alternated roles so all parents could attend without child care concerns.

We do not want to give the impression that our reach-out efforts have been rather easy to develop and implement. We made quite a few errors and got discouraged at many turns in the process. We have, however, achieved some satisfying results. We plan to continue trying new ways to improve our attraction of hard-to-reach clients, as well as developing new methods for solving other service-delivery problems.

Chapter 6
Evaluating Your Effectiveness

Evaluation scares people. Some imagine it as too complicated. Others criticize it as too academic. Still others oppose it as not applicable to the kind of treatment they provide. A few resist evaluation for fear of finding out their weaknesses. Many argue that evaluation is nice — when you have the extra time and money. This chapter provides you with some easy-to-use methods to evaluate economically and conveniently the effectiveness of the treatments you employ. Evaluation should be thought of as something more than a frill, to be done only when everything else has already been done; instead, we argue that the provision and maintenance of quality services, and your growth as a professional, depend on systematic, accurate evaluation.

What Is Evaluation?

Evaluation means nothing more than determining the worth of something by careful study. We constantly evaluate things in daily life. When we dine out, we comment on the food, "This is the best cheeseburger I've had"; the service, "They sure are slow with my iced tea"; and the surroundings, "The busboy better get busy. The tables are covered with empty trays." All of these comments indicate our evaluations of the dining experience. When we make a large purchase, we evaluate the wisdom of our choice, "The gas mileage in this car is better, and the safety and frequency of repair records look good also." We often share the results of our evaluations with others: "The last time I ate there, I got food poisoning." "I've had nothing but bad luck with my car since I bought it. You can bet I'll never buy another one like that."

Some of our evaluations take more time and thought than others; some of our evaluations are more correct than others. Any evaluation we make is influenced not only by the product we're evaluating, the restaurant or the automobile in our examples, but by many other variables as well. For example, if we've been out of the country for a month and haven't had a hamburger, our first McDonald's may receive an especially favorable evaluation. If we've spent $10,000 on a new car, we might find it difficult to admit the car is a lemon and we've been taken. Understanding what influences our evaluations, and taking steps to see that our evaluations are predicated on careful study, can serve to make our evaluations more accurate and more useful to us.

Why Evaluation Is Important

By far the most important rationale for engaging in evaluation is that it lets you see exactly the gains your parents are or are not making. For example, if you keep track of how often Mrs. Watts praises Crystal, you'll be able to see if her rate increases. If it does, terrific, you can then focus on your next treatment objective. If, on the other hand, the rate of praise decreases or shows no change, you'll know that the methods you've used haven't worked: A change in treatment is necessary. Without the careful study required by evaluation, and the information produced by evaluation, you may continue to use ineffective methods simply because they are comfortable or because you "believe" they work. This in turn means the people who seek out your service may receive snake oil. Evaluation gives you the feedback required to modify the treatment you provide to better meet the needs of your families.

Aside from the potential immediate benefits to your clients, evaluation accomplishes other important objectives. If you determine that your treatment of a particular family has produced significant changes, evaluation methods allow for the transmission of results and the description of effective procedures between workers. You can share your findings with co-workers who may then attempt to achieve the same results with their families. These replications help to take practice out of the realm of mystery and subject it to scientific scrutiny. If you evaluate your practice, you can share your results not only with your co-workers, but also with other professionals at conferences and with members of the scientific community. Finally, documentations of effectiveness are useful to determine staff salaries and promotions and to convince funding sources of the worth of the services.

Arguments Against Evaluation

Many professionals who work with parents argue that evaluation takes too much time from already full schedules. Without question, the majority of family practitioners carry huge and demanding caseloads and, of course, evaluation does take time. Consider, though, the following: Few would dispute that at least some of what we do with families does not work. Some parents conclude treatment facing exactly the same problems as when they started. The accuracy of this statement lends support for devoting at least a small portion of time to evaluation activities. If some assurance exists that evaluation will, in the long run, help us to provide more efficient, effective service, and to reduce the number of families for whom service fails, then a strong case can be made for serving fewer families, or for at least delaying the provision of services, to permit additional time for practice evaluation. Evaluation methods range from the extremely complex, requiring full-time staff, computers, and hundreds of subjects, to the relatively simple, requiring no extra manpower, minimal interruption of service, and little extra time. Numerous variables, including agency commitment to evaluation, influence the type and extent of evaluation you will have the opportunity to execute.

A frequently heard comment is, "Much of what I do in my practice can't be evaluated, but I know the parents I work with get better." Surely, some of what we do with parents is difficult to define, measure, and evaluate. Perhaps the most difficult obstacle to overcome in evaluation, though, is not defining or measuring the service we provide, but rather our own reluctance to even engage in the evaluation process. This reluctance can be explained in part because of a lack of training, comfort, or familiarity with what is involved in evaluation, and by a sincere concern that priority be given to providing service to parents.

With a commitment to evaluation, you can get the training necessary to evaluate your work. Several excellent texts describe in detail practical evaluation methods (see, for example, Bloom & Fischer, 1982), and most major conferences provide workshops or papers on clinical evaluation methods. Once you've given evaluation a try or two, you'll find your apprehension decreases (in fact, if the case outcome is favorable, you may even enjoy the process!), your skill and comfort at applying and adapting various evaluation methods to your situations increases, and you'll be better able to select and implement treatment strategies best suited for each family.

In crisis situations where practice and evaluation seem incompatible, simply recognize that as a practitioner your priority must always be the provision of service. Of course, if this situation repeats itself frequently, you should consider steps to minimize its recurrence or to incorporate evaluation methods into crisis intervention.

One concern shared by many practitioners is that evaluation requires them to employ a certain treatment modality, usually described as behavioral. Related to this concern is that evaluation introduces artificiality and a mechanical nature to the treatment process. Both of these concerns are unfortunate because neither need be correct. True, some methodologies lend themselves more to evaluation than others: Those designed to affect observable events, those with clearly specifiable procedures, and those producing rapid results. However, the purpose of evaluation is to determine if the procedures you use, regardless of their theoretical origins, produce the outcomes you desire. The purpose of evaluation is not to force you to select a particular theoretical approach or treatment strategy ahead of time — that is, before you've evaluated your first choice. Of course, if you select a treatment, introduce and evaluate it, and find unsatisfactory results, you would then want to revise your treatment. Evaluation need not, and should not, affect the nature or characteristics of the treatment you provide. Obviously, the outcome must affect your treatment or you will have wasted both your time and that of your clients. The solution comes with familiarity and practice with the wide array of evaluation methods available. It is equally important to assess your effectiveness if your treatment approach is psychoanalytic, behavioral, eclectic, or somewhere in between. As you practice evaluating the service you deliver, you'll find that you can design your evaluation system to fit within, rather than to define, the parameters of your treatment, and that you can reduce mechanical or artificial constraints.

EVALUATION METHODS

Evaluation consists of two main components, a measurement system and an experimental design. The methods you use to keep track of those client characteristics, thoughts, feelings, and behaviors you're interested in comprise the measurement system. For example, you may want to *measure* how often Mr. Vecsey asks Rachel about her schoolwork, how likely Mr. Canyon is to sexually abuse his stepdaughter, how Michael feels about school, or how regularly Ms. Griffen uses the skills you've been teaching her. The measurement system you design for a particular parent may measure several dimensions: You may ask Mrs. Jason to jot down every time David has a tantrum; you may ask her to complete a pencil-and-paper inventory to determine the extent of her depression; and you may observe her interactions with her son while the two of them play a parlor game. The measurement system provides you with the feedback you must have to make sound treatment decisions and to assess the effectiveness of the treatment you provide.

The experimental design provides a set of logical rules that tell you when to begin delivering service and when to employ the measurement system. It helps you determine whether any changes picked up by the measurement system are due to the treatment you've introduced or to something else that happened at the same time. A wide variety of experimental designs are available; each has its own strengths and weaknesses. For a comprehensive review of experimental designs, refer to Barlow and Hersen (1984).

The key to all evaluation is a *comparison level*. Clinical evaluation involves comparing the characteristics, thoughts, feelings, and behaviors of the client before treatment with those same characteristics, thoughts, feelings, and behaviors during or after treatment. You're interested in a comparison between client performance during and after treatment with the performance of the same client before treatment. This differs significantly from other types of research that compares two groups of clients: one group that received the treatment compared with a second group that did not receive the treatment, or that received a different type of treatment. For a clinician this later type of research generally produces results that are of little usefulness. In our earlier examples, you'd compare how often before treatment Mr. Vecsey asks Rachel about her schoolwork with how often he asks her during or after treatment. You'd compare how suicidal Mr. Canyon was before treatment with how suicidal he was during or after treatment. Similarly, you'd compare how Michael feels about school before and after treatment, and how regularly before treatment Ms. Griffen used the skills you'd been teaching compared with her use after treatment.

Considerable useful information can be obtained just by using a measurement system, without an experimental design. You can make much progress toward evaluating the effectiveness of the treatments you use simply by introducing a measurement system. Your measurement system shows you if change has occurred, and the magnitude of the change. It also tells you if change has not occurred. If change has not occurred, you can correctly conclude that your treatment failed, at least with regard to the particular dimensions you chose to measure.

Without an experimental design, though, a measurement system alone is insufficient to conclude that a change is due to the treatment, that your treatment caused the change. Any of a million other things might have been responsible. Perhaps Mr. Vecsey now asks Rachel about her schoolwork more frequently not because of the treatment but because Rachel is no longer in soccer so he has nothing else to ask her about. Or maybe Mr. Canyon isn't quite so depressed because his boss, who was always giving him a hard time, got transferred to Siberia. Maybe Michael likes school more now because he's decided to become an engineer and realizes school is a necessary prerequisite, and Ms. Griffen is using her parenting skills more than before because child welfare told her if she kept beating on her kids the state would take them away. The measurement system gives you the information you need in order to have a comparison level, to determine if change occurred, to determine the amount of change, and to determine if your treatment failed. If changes do occur, the experimental design helps you to conclude that your treatment, and not other events occurring in the client's life, was responsible for the change.

TYPES OF MEASURES

A variety of measures may be taken to evaluate your effectiveness with parents. The more commonly employed measures include: parent self-reports, standardized checklists and scales, parent satisfaction questionnaires, analogues or role-play exercises, collateral contacts, structured observations in the treatment setting, and direct observation in the home or school. Each of these is briefly discussed below.

Parent-self reports: One especially convenient way to assess your effectiveness is simply to ask the parents for feedback. Although this method has many limitations, if collected properly parent self-reports can provide much useful information. Parent self-reports may be either verbal, as in the form of an interview, or written, as in the form of a weekly homework assignment. Entire textbooks are devoted to interviewing skills and to standardized checklists and scales, clearly making such complex topics beyond the scope of this overview. Acquaint yourself with the guidelines described here to help you collect as accurate information as possible from parents.

Ask both general and specific questions. For example, you might start out by asking, "Has Johnny's behavior changed since you've been in this program?" Then, after the parents have answered, follow up with specific questions: "About how often is Johnny having temper tantrums now?" The general questions help you to cover all areas that might be of concern to parents, including areas you might otherwise overlook. General questions give parents a chance to bring up anything that may be of concern to them. The specific questions help you to refine the information you are collecting and to minimize distortion. For example, a parent may say, "Yes, Johnny is behaving better," but upon further investigation you may find that his temper tantrums have actually increased! Such disparities highlight areas requiring additional exploration. It's also a good idea to include several open-ended questions that solicit general feedback from the parents. For example, a comment like, "Well, we've covered a lot of information today. Are there any other topics you'd like to discuss? Or, is there anything else on your mind that we need to cover here?" can sometimes provide a springboard for a wealth of information.

Secondly, try to avoid loading the questions in your favor. For example, a question like, "Johnny sure is behaving better now than he was before, isn't he?" is more likely to compel the parents to answer "yes" than a question phrased like, "Has Johnny's behavior changed in the last few weeks?" Don't make the parents feel you want a particular answer: Remember, the only correct answer is the accurate one, regardless of whether it's what you would like to hear. One good way to check yourself on this is to ask for the same information in two or more different ways and compare the results. For example, early in the interview you might say, "Any changes in Donia's tantrums?" Later, you might ask, "Is Donia having fewer tantrums than when we first started?" or "Donia was having about 11 tantrums per week.

About how many is she having now?" The answers should agree. If they don't you may need to check how you're asking the questions and follow up with the parents to clarify the discrepancy. The problem may be insensitivity in your measurement system, biased questioning, misunderstanding from the parents, or a variety of factors. Follow-up questioning from you will help to insure the accuracy of the information you collect from parents.

One easy mistake to make is to differentially encourage or discourage replies from parents depending on whether the replies are consistent with your expectations or desired outcomes. For example:

> Parent: Yes, Johnny has really improved lately. He hasn't had a fight with his sister in over a week.
> Therapist: That's absolutely fantastic. You all are really doing a great job.
> Parent: Thanks. But he has started to beat up a lot of the other kids in the neighborhood and now they won't play with him. We're really worried.
> Therapist: Oh, it's nothing to worry about. Boys will be boys. I bet his sister is much happier now that he isn't picking on her.

Let the parents know you are equally interested in any information they may provide. If you show disappointment at reports of no change or increased problems, the parents may start providing you with glowing, but inaccurate, reports.

Written self-reports from parents may avoid some of the potential biasing factors present in interviews. If you ask the parents to record their reports at the time the event occurs, the information will be less subject to distortion due to the passage of time. Furthermore, you can write instructions on the recording form to help the parents remember precisely what to record. Written assignments may prompt parents to think about their work with you at times between visits, and they may encourage parents to be specific in their reporting.

Parents may require assistance and support from you to routinely comply with your request that they collect self-report information. You can take several steps to increase their understanding of the importance of your requests and their compliance rate. First, make certain your request is specific. An offhanded general comment like, "Keep track of times when Johnny upsets you" is much less likely to be taken seriously than a specific instruction like, "Whenever Johnny upsets you and you start to lose your temper, write down the time, date, what he was doing that got you upset, and how you handled it." You can make your request even more specific by writing it down on a recording form and including an example or two. Ask the parent to recall the last time Johnny got her upset, and enter her recollection as the example on the recording form. Get an acknowledgment from the parent that she understands the request and ask her to paraphrase the request back to you.

Evaluating Your Effectiveness

> Practitioner: Okay, Mrs. French, do you understand what it is we're trying to keep track of? Can you go ahead and explain it to me so I'm sure we're both talking about the same thing?
> Mrs. French: Whenever Johnny does something that gets me really angry and upset, like when he dragged the bag of charcoal from the garage across the living room and out to the patio, I should record on this form what Johnny did, when, and how I responded. Right?"
> Practitioner: "Right. Do you have any questions?"

Always ask the parent if she has any questions about the assignment. Her reply may not only tell you about her questions but also about any reservations she has. Now is the time to deal with these, rather than next week when she returns without the information you need to make good treatment decisions, or worse yet, when she doesn't return at all.

Providing sound, personalized rationales will also help to motivate parents to collect self-report data. Let them know what benefits they can expect to gain if they do collect the information and the obstacles that may be faced in the absence of the information.

> Practitioner: Ms. Franks, the information I'm asking you to collect is very important because with it we can see if Bertha continues to fight with the neighborhood children and if the methods we try are working. That will help us help Bertha make friends more quickly and learn to play more friendly with others. Without it, we'll have to make a lot more guesses about what's going on and I suspect we'll move much slower.
> Ms. Franks: I understand, and I want to get this problem resolved as quickly as possible. I hate to see Bertha so unhappy.

Finally, making the assignment clear and obtaining a commitment just starts the process. To keep it going, you must also always follow through by beginning each meeting with a review of the parent self-report data from the previous week. This sets the expectation that the information is to be collected and reinforces to the parent the importance of the information. If the parent has completed the assignment, sincere encouragement is in order: "Terrific, Mrs. Jessie, looks like you've really taken care to complete the recording form every day — and accurately, too." If the parent arrives without the form, a comment of understanding is appropriate ("Sometimes it's hard to get everything done during the week that we need to"), but balanced with renewed emphasis about the need for the information ("Even though it is rough, we really do need to have the recording form completed"). Ask recalcitrant offenders to complete the form from recollection, and for those few parents who repeatedly fail to complete the assignment, explore with them the difficulties they are having. Ultimately, if they cannot assist you in the collection of the information you need to make thoughtful, effective treatment decisions, we recommend that you refer them to an alternative service.

Parent self-report measures represent a tricky source of data. On the one hand, they represent a sort of bottom-line measure: If the parent doesn't report success, perhaps no other measure is important. On the other hand, many variables, in addition to the specific treatment you provide, influence parent self-reports. Determining exactly what a favorable report reflects is problematic at best. This seeming paradox argues then for the use of corroborative measures when relying on parent self-reports.

Standardized checklists and scales: A wide variety of checklists and scales are available to assess the effects of your services. Scales or checklists are available to measure everything from parent attitudes toward their children, parent levels of self-confidence, depression, and marital satisfaction, to child behavior problems, adjustment in school, self-concept, and perceived locus of control. Standardized checklists and scales are especially convenient and easy to use: Many include detailed instructions for scoring and interpretation and have been tested for reliability and validity. Furthermore, by using a standardized instrument you may be able to compare your findings with those of others who have used the same measurement instruments: Your findings will have some compatibility with existing literature. Standardized instruments sometimes avoid many of the biasing influences operating during interviews, and parents may find it easier to respond critically to a written question than in face-to-face conversation. However, standardized scales and checklists do have their own set of limitations. Some parents may not understand the language used by the instrument, or the required reading level may be too high. Or two parents may interpret the same questions very differently. Parents may also respond in ways they think are socially desirable, or only in extremes (that is, always marking either the 1 or the 7 on a 7-point scale). Another disadvantage with standardized scales and checklists is that they may not lend themselves to repeated administrations. If this is the case, you can ask the parent to complete the forms infrequently, say at the beginning and at the end of the treatment. This limits your ability to use the information for the family, because you won't receive it until the conclusion of treatment. Finally, the standardized instruments may not measure the precise effects of your treatment, but instead be sensitive to more global changes. For example, you may be able to see a difference in Mrs. Jones' overall attitude toward her son, but you may not be able to determine what particular new parenting skill or combination of skills were responsible for this change.

In our work, we frequently use the Parent Attitudes Test (Cowen, Huser, Beach, & Rappaport, 1970), which measures parent perceptions of child adjustment. This instrument has been shown to be reliable and valid (Cowen et al., 1970), and to differentiate clinic from nonclinic children (Forehand, King, Peed, & Yoder, 1975). The Parent Attitudes Test is available from

Emory & Cowen, Psychology Department, University of Rochester, Rochester, New York 14627. We use the instrument once during our initial interview with each family, once after session 8, and at the annual follow-up visit.

Parent-satisfaction questionnaires: A third convenient method to assess your effectiveness is to use parent-satisfaction questionnaires. These are similar to parent self-report measures and standardized checklists in that you are asking the parents for their opinions about the service you've provided. However, they differ in that they are typically administered anonymously. Parent-satisfaction questionnaires require less of your time because parents complete them on their own, either at the treatment setting or at home. Data from parent-satisfaction questionnaires can be collapsed from several parents to provide a summary of your effectiveness and to highlight areas requiring your attention. A word of caution, though: Parents often respond according to what they think you would like to see. They may report that their child's behavior is improved, that they enjoyed the program, and that they'd recommend it to friends, when in fact none of these responses reflect the actual situation. You can combat this in part by discussing with the parents ahead of time the importance of accurate reporting and objectivity and assuring them of the anonymity of their replies. Again, these risks support the notion of corroborative measures. In addition to Consumer Satisfaction Questionnaires, some other measure is necessary to confirm or refute your findings.

Analogues or role plays: Analogues or role plays provide an opportunity for you to observe how the parents respond under a given set of circumstances. Although they are one step removed from real life, they do require parents to demonstrate behavior. You get to see what the parents can and cannot do. We use role plays designed to measure parents' proficiency with each of the skills we aim to teach: praise and attention, rewards and privileges, suggestive praise, ignoring, time-out, removing rewards and privileges, spanking, and compliance. When constructing role plays, keep the scenario as close to the family's situation as possible. It's usually necessary to have several prepared for each skill for each age group. A role play for the parent of a 3-year-old won't work for the parent of a 12-year-old.

We use role plays to monitor parent progress after each lesson and at the conclusion of training. If we are working in a group, one parent plays the part of the child, one parent performs as the parent. If you are working with one parent, you may play the child or you may ask the parent to pretend the child is present. The parent receives the role-play description sheet and is asked to follow the instructions. No additional information is provided. In this way, we can see just how close the parent is to mastery of the skill without any extra assistance.

Parent performance on role-play exercises can be evaluated in several ways. A cursory, but easily obtained, measure is simply to score each parent response as *yes* or *no*, the parent did or did not demonstrate the skill. A slightly more complicated system involves assigning some qualitative judgment to the performance, as described in Chapter 4. For example, you might watch a given performance and score it using a 5-point scale, with 1 representing extremely poor performance and 5 representing outstanding performance. Although this system introduces more room for error or differences of opinion, it provides more description of what the parents have mastered.

Collateral contacts: Another way to assess your effectiveness is to contact individuals familiar with your families. For example, teachers, neighbors, clergy, daycare workers, babysitters, and grandparents can describe changes in the families. When you obtain reports from collateral contacts, follow the same guidelines recommended for asking the parents directly to avoid biasing the information you collect. Before contacting collaterals, consider any repercussions that might occur. For example, some individuals may react adversely to a child or parent's being involved in parenting classes or treatment and may behave inappropriately to the child or parent. Be sure to obtain written permission from the family before contacting anyone. Once you've collected information from collaterals, discuss any incongruity between reports from parents and reports from collaterals with the parents. Disparities may be due to inaccurate reporting from collaterals or parents, or to changes in the child or parent behavior occurring inconsistently across settings.

Direct observation in the home: Direct observation of parent-child interactions in the home may provide the most accurate and valid picture of the nature of the parent-child relationship. When executed properly, direct observation leaves little room for subjectivity or distortion. How complicated, expensive, or time consuming the collection of observation data need be depends on how you intend to use the information. Some sophisticated research uses observational data systems that require extensive time, training, and staff. On the other hand, practitioners can collect observational data that are tremendously helpful to assess both treatment process and outcome, yet which are relatively economical and inexpensive, particularly when considered in terms of their contributions.

We collect in-home observational data on all families that participate in our program. We observe those families involved in our research a minimum of three times before and six times during treatment. For those families who are not participating in our research, but who are receiving the service, we collect observational data at least three times: once before treatment, once during treatment, and once towards the end of treatment. Follow-up observational visits are conducted 3 and 12 months after treatment. We conduct 45-minute observations at times convenient for the parents. Parent and child may be engaged in any activity, alone or together, ranging from preparing a meal, to playing soccer, to watching television. We attempt to capture a representative slice of the parent-child interaction. In clinical practice the most practical observational system to use is a simple frequency count of those parenting skills and child behaviors you're interested in measuring.

When you first introduce the idea of observing in the home, expect parents to express reservations or discomfort. To alleviate their concerns, provide them with two important rationales about the usefulness of your visit: First, visits provide you an opportunity to better understand their situation, and second, they give you feedback about the effectiveness of the service so you can make any necessary changes. You should also explain that you will come at times convenient for them, that you aren't expecting them to "perform," in fact, that you want them to behave as they normally would, and that they should consider you "invisible" when you are there. Explain that you aren't allowed to talk to them, nor they to you, once you've started recording and that they should try to remain in sight and hearing of you. You can also reassure them that after the first visit or two they will feel more relaxed. Once you and they give it a try, you'll find this to be exactly the case: You'll both feel more comfortable and you'll realize the importance of direct observation in the home.

Characteristics of a Good Measurement System

Strive for a measurement system that is reliable, valid, and manageable. Think of a reliable measurement system as one that is accurate; a valid system as one that measures what you intend it to measure; and a manageable system as one that provides you with sufficient information to make sound treatment decisions but that doesn't interfere with the delivery of services.

At least one of your measures should be used *repeatedly*, at least three times before and three or more times during or after treatment. If you use a measure at least three times before treatment you will usually have enough information to make a prediction about what would have happened to the characteristics, thoughts, feelings, and behaviors had you not introduced any service. If you use a measure fewer than three times before treatment, your ability to make accurate predictions will be limited. Repeated measurement gives you the comparison level required to conduct an evaluation.

In addition to using at least one measure repeatedly before and during or after treatment, a complete measurement system employs multiple measures or several different measures. For example, you might use direct in-home observation to evaluate how often Mr. Wright praises his daughter and how often she completes her chores; role-play exercises to see if he has mastered the steps in time-out; and a standardized questionnaire to assess his attitudes and perceptions. You are interested in evaluating many aspects of Mr. Wright's relationship with his daughter; multiple measures allow you to use the measurement tool best suited to assess each aspect.

We have used a variety of measurement systems with our families. Described here is a sample complete package that you may use as a model to design a measurement system suitable for your objectives.

Direct observation: Collect in-home observational data three times prior to starting treatment, once after teaching praise, once after teaching ignoring, and once after teaching compliance. Do a follow-up visit within 12 weeks.

Role-play: After each new skill, ask the parent to demonstrate correct use during role-play exercises.

Collateral contacts: Confirm parent reports of child improvement by contacting referral source and/or school.

Standardized questionnaire: Administer the Parent Attitudes Test before the first skill and within 3 weeks after the last skill.

Parent self-report: Collect weekly self-support data using Practice Records.

EXPERIMENTAL DESIGNS

The experimental design helps you to determine if changes detected by your measurement system are due to the service you've provided or if they may be due to other events that have occurred. Without an experimental design you can't be sure that your treatment *caused* the improvements. Countless books exist that describe various experimental designs and their strengths and weaknesses. For your purposes as a practitioner, two designs are especially suitable, the *A–B design* and the *multiple baseline design*.

A–B design: In this design, the A letter represents time before the beginning of treatment, before the parent started receiving services from you. The B

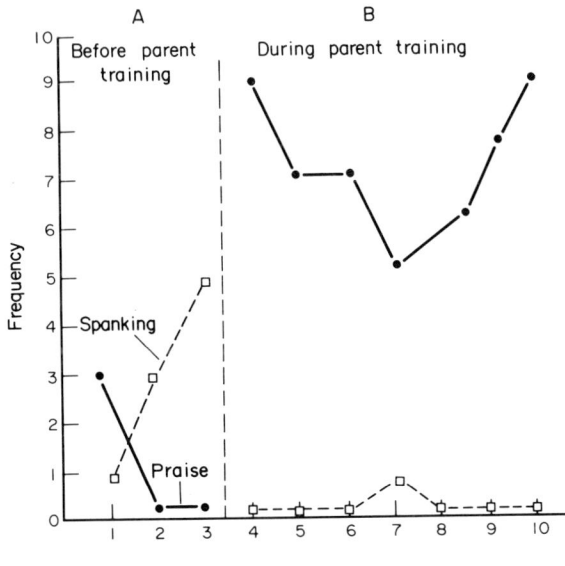

FIGURE 6.1. Simple A-B experimental design, showing frequency of praise and spanking before and after parent training.

represents time during and after services began. The A-B experimental design requires repeated measurement under both the A (before treatment) and the B (during and after treatment) condition. Figure 6.1 illustrates data collected within an A-B experimental design framework. Under the A condition we can see that Ms. Fett praised her son about once per day and spanked him about 3 times per day. Under the B condition, after Ms. Fett began treatment, she started to praise her son about 7 times per day and only spanked him once over seven weeks. The dotted lines shown in the B condition illustrate your prediction about how often praising and spanking would have occurred had Ms. Fett not participated in your service. You can use this line as a comparison level: Considerable difference exists between your prediction and what actually occurred. The question then becomes, was my service responsible for this difference?

Unfortunately, the A-B design is limited in its ability to let you answer this question. Any of a variety of events may have occurred at about the same time as your service. Perhaps Ms. Fett joined a church group that advocated not using spanking but using praise. Perhaps she finally believed her mother when her mother said, "You can catch more flies with honey than with vinegar." The A-B design does not let you rule out these other events as possible causes for the observed change. Nevertheless, it is a very useful design because it does let you see (a) if change has occurred, (b) the magnitude of the change, and (c) if your treatment failed.

You can strengthen the conclusions you may draw from an A-B design in two ways: by conducting a supplemental inquiry and by conducting a replication. A supplemental inquiry involves asking the client to identify other events occurring at about the same time as the treatment that the client thinks might be responsible for the change. For example, your supplemental inquiry with Ms. Fett might sound like this:

> Practitioner: Ms. Fett, there has been a major change in how you relate to your son. You now praise him frequently and almost never spank him. Why do you suppose this change occurred?
>
> Ms. Fett: Well, I've been trying to do the things we've been practicing here and he seems to really enjoy them and his behavior is better.
>
> Practitioner: It's great that you've been trying the skills we've been covering. Can you think of anything else that has been happening that might be responsible for the change?
>
> Ms. Fett: Well, I was having a lot of difficulty at work with my boss and felt under a lot of pressure. It was really difficult for me to praise and I was real quick to lose my temper with my son. But I now have a new boss, in fact he started right after I started this program. He's very patient and kind and I'm much more relaxed and patient with David. The little things he does that used to drive me crazy don't bother me at all any more.
>
> Practitioner: I'm glad to hear you've got a pleasant boss. That can really make a difference. Were you familiar with the skills we've talked about here before you started?
>
> Ms. Fett: Some, but I didn't really know how to use them exactly. I've learned that here and I've learned the importance of follow-through and consistency. New boss or not, I've gotten that much for sure from here.

From this supplemental inquiry, the practitioner can see that the service likely accomplished some change, but that other external events also made substantial contributions.

A replication involves repeating the same service with a different client and evaluating the results. You will be using the same experimental design, an A-B design, and most likely the same or very similar measurement system. If the results resemble those obtained with the first client, support is added that the service, and not the other events, was responsible for the change. Each replication that produces similar results strengthens the conclusion that the service produced the change. Repeating the process six times, each time using an A-B design, provides more evidence than repeating the process five times. You may also conduct a supplemental inquiry with each replication for further proof regarding the effects of your intervention.

Multiple baseline design: The second type of experimental design that lends itself to clinical practice is called a multiple baseline design. The multiple baseline design represents an extension of the A-B design in that it consists of

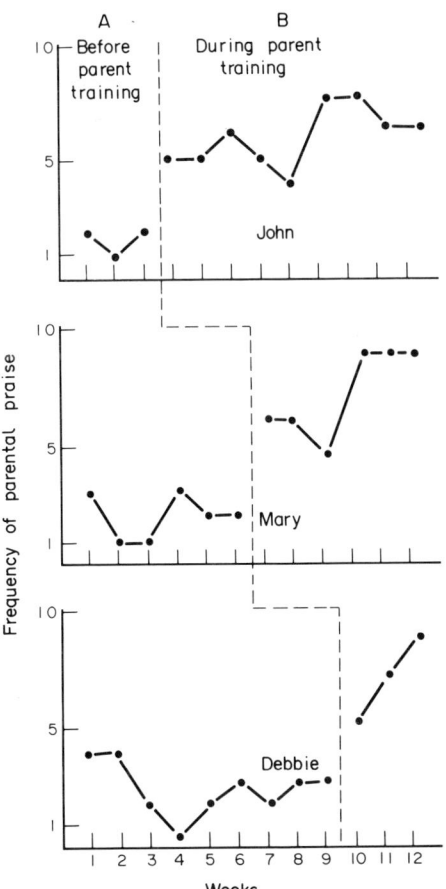

FIGURE 6.2. Multiple Baseline Design Across Subjects, showing frequency of parental praise under two experimental conditions: (A) before parent training and (B) during parent training.

two or more A–B designs, each referred to as a leg of the multiple baseline design. Figure 6.2 shows a three-legged multiple baseline design. You can see that each leg consists of both an A and a B condition, just like in the A–B design. The main characteristic that distinguishes the multiple baseline design is the staggered starting dates for treatment. In the illustration, the dashed verticle line marks the point at which treatment began. You can see that for John, shown on the first leg of the design, treatment began at session 4; for Mary, shown on the second leg of the design, treatment began at session 7; and for Debbie, shown on the third leg of the design, treatment began at session 10.

The multiple baseline design is considered a much stronger design than the A–B design because it helps to determine if events other than the service are responsible for the change. Because the multiple baseline design uses a staggered starting date, if the treatment, and only the treatment, is responsible for the change, then you would not expect to see any change until the treatment is introduced. Thus, if you start treatment for John, changes should be seen only on the first leg of the multiple baseline design; no change should be seen for Mary or for Debbie. Mary and Debbie serve as a kind of control for John. Then, when you introduce the treatment for Mary, changes should be seen only on the second leg of the multiple baseline design, no change should be seen for Debbie. Finally, when you introduce the treatment for Debbie, changes should be seen on the third leg of the multiple baseline design. What you end up with then is one A–B design showing an effect, with John, and two replications of this effect, one with Mary and the other with Debbie. In addition, Mary and Debbie have served as a control for John, and Debbie as a control for Mary. The multiple baseline design provides strong evidence that observed changes are due to your treatment, not due to other events.

The multiple baseline design may be used across individuals, across settings or environments, or across behaviors. For example, you might be interested in Johnny's behavior at home, at school, and at daycare. Each setting could provide one leg of the multiple baseline design. Or you might be interested in Johnny's temper tantrums, fights, and crying episodes, with each behavior shown on a separate leg of the multiple baseline.

The multiple baseline design is not limited to use with a single individual. You may include as many individuals as you'd like. For example, you may be offering your parenting services to three separate groups of parents, with 10 families in each group. To use a multiple baseline design, each group would appear as a leg in the design.

The major limitations of the various types of multiple baseline designs (across individuals, settings, or behaviors) include the necessity of having all subjects ready to begin treatment at the same time, yet temporarily delaying treatment for some subjects, and the possibility that changes produced by the treatment may show up either across settings or across behaviors before the treatment has been introduced.

EVALUATION AS AN ONGOING PROCESS

Perhaps the most important point to remember about clinical evaluation is that it is an ongoing process. Evaluation is not an event that occurs primarily after the fact; at that point you don't have an opportunity to correct your course with your client. Never forget your primary objective in evaluation: to improve the quality of service you provide to your clients. Use a measurement system and an experimental design as tools to help you accomplish this objective.

Afterword

You're ready now to organize your first group and try out your new skills. Helping parents learn new ways to interact with children presents intense challenges, disappointments, and satisfactions. Hearing a parent say, "Rosalind is a different kid now. I used to dread coming home from work because it just meant another fight. Now, she's fun to be around. I actually enjoy spending time with her," lets you know your work has paid off. Hearing a parent say, "Derrick is still driving me nuts. He was kicked out of school and the neighbors won't let him play with their kids. I just don't know what to do," provides the motivation to continue the search for effective parenting skills.

No single program can possibly provide parents with all they need to know — thank goodness. The diversity in parenting styles no doubt contributes to the diversity in children and adults that makes our world so delightful. When children behave in ways that rob them of their opportunities to experience harmonious relationships with their parents and with others in society, we have a compelling obligation to deliver prompt, effective service. The methods described in this book will get you started.

Appendix A
Practice Records

Practice Record
Lesson 1: PRAISE and ATTENTION

Name_____

The practice assignment for this week is to:
praise 10 times every day.

Instructions: Every time you praise, put a check (✓) in one of the boxes for that day.

	1	2	3	4	5	6	7	8	9	10
Sunday										
Monday										
Tuesday										
Wednesday										
Thursday										
Friday										
Saturday										

Teaching Child Management Skills

Practice Record
Lesson 2: REWARDS and PRIVILEGES

Name_____

The practice assignment for this week is to:
give 2 rewards or privileges every day.

Instructions: Every time you give a reward or privilege, put a check (✓) in one of the boxes for that day.

	1	2
Sunday		
Monday		
Tuesday		
Wednesday		
Thursday		
Friday		
Saturday		

Appendix A

Practice Record
Lesson 3: SUGGESTIVE PRAISE

Name_____

The practice assignment for this week is to:
use suggestive praise 5 times each day.

Instructions: Every time you use suggestive praise, put a check (✓) in one of the boxes for that day.

	1	2	3	4	5
Sunday					
Monday					
Tuesday					
Wednesday					
Thursday					
Friday					
Saturday					

Practice Record
Lesson 4: IGNORING

Name_____

The practice assignment for this week is to:
ignore annoying behaviors every day for a 1-hour period.
Pick an hour when you're sure your child will be around.

Instructions: Every time during the practice hour when you ignore your child's annoying behavior, put a check (✓) in the box for that day.

Sunday	
Monday	
Tuesday	
Wednesday	
Thursday	
Friday	
Saturday	

Appendix A

Practice Record
Lesson 5: TIME-OUT

Name_____

The practice assignment for this week is to:
use time-out any time your child does a serious misbehavior.

Instructions: Every time you use time-out with your child, put a check (✓) in the box for that day.

Sunday	
Monday	
Tuesday	
Wednesday	
Thursday	
Friday	
Saturday	

Teaching Child Management Skills

Practice Record
Lesson 6: REMOVING REWARDS and PRIVILEGES

Name_____

The practice assignment for this week is to:
remove a reward or privilege any time your child misbehaves.

Instructions: Every time you remove a reward or privilege put a check (✓) in the box for that day.

Sunday	
Monday	
Tuesday	
Wednesday	
Thursday	
Friday	
Saturday	

Appendix A

Practice Record
Lesson 7: PHYSICAL PUNISHMENT
(optional)

Name_____

The practice assignment for this week is to:
use physical punishment *only* for dangerous behaviors.

Instructions: If you use physical punishment this week put a check (✓) in the box for that day.

Sunday	
Monday	
Tuesday	
Wednesday	
Thursday	
Friday	
Saturday	

Practice Record
Lesson 8: COMPLIANCE

Name_____

The practice assignment for this week is to:
1. give 2 instructions every day.
2. if your child does as you ask, follow through with praise or rewards and privileges.
3. if your child does not do as you ask, follow through with time-out or removal of rewards and privileges.

Instructions: Every time you give an instruction and follow through, put a check (✓) in the box for that day. Also put a check (✓) if you followed through with praise or rewards, or with time-out or removal of rewards.

	Instructions	Praise or Reward	Time-out/ Removal of Rewards
Sunday	1.		
	2.		
Monday	1.		
	2.		
Tuesday	1.		
	2.		
Wednesday	1.		
	2.		
Thursday	1.		
	2.		
Friday	1.		
	2.		
Saturday	1.		
	2.		

Appendix B
Key Points of the Basic Skills

KEY POINTS TO REMEMBER ABOUT PRAISE AND ATTENTION

1. Use praise and attention only during or immediately after behavior you want to happen more often.
2. Withhold praise and attention when children misbehave.
3. Make your praise descriptive.
4. Include positive comments and encouragement in your praise.
5. Give praise for minor appropriate behavior.
6. Make your praise sincere.
7. Use physical affection with praise.
8. Fit praise to each child's likes and dislikes.
9. Vary praise each time you use it.

KEY POINTS TO REMEMBER ABOUT REWARDS AND PRIVILEGES

1. Present rewards and privileges only during or immediately after desired behavior.
2. Do not use rewards and privileges to stop misbehavior.
3. Accompany rewards and privileges with descriptions of the rewarded behavior.
4. Use positive and encouraging words when giving rewards and privileges.
5. Physical affection should often accompany rewards and privileges.
6. Parents should use the nice things they already do as rewards and privileges.
7. Rewards and privileges should vary each time they are used.
8. Individualize rewards and privileges for children's likes and dislikes.
9. Give rewards and privileges in proportion to the importance and difficulty of behavior.
10. Occasionally tell children ahead of time what they can do to earn rewards and privileges.

Appendix B

KEY POINTS TO REMEMBER ABOUT SUGGESTIVE PRAISE

1. Suggestive praise requires phrases such as "for not," "instead of," or "without."
2. Suggestive praise should be given when children are not misbehaving.
3. Suggestive praise must be descriptive.
4. Suggestive praise must be sincere.
5. Sometimes combine suggestive praise with praise and attention.
6. Sometimes combine suggestive praise with physical affection.
7. Sometimes include rewards and privileges with suggestive praise.
8. Suggestive praise should be individualized.
9. Vary suggestive praise each time you use it.

KEY POINTS TO REMEMBER ABOUT IGNORING

1. Whenever your children are doing something that seems to be for your attention and you would like them to stop, ignore them.
2. Use ignoring each time the bothersome behavior occurs.
3. When you ignore a problem, it may get worse before it gets better.
4. Do something distracting to help you ignore.
5. Use suggestive praise with ignoring.

Appendix B
KEY POINTS TO REMEMBER ABOUT TIME-OUT

1. Use time-out to decrease dangerous or serious problems.
2. Always use a dull area for time-out.
3. Use time-out only during or immediately after the behavior you want to decrease.
4. Keep attention to a minimum during time-out.
5. Children should be kept in time-out briefly.
6. Praise children for the first desirable thing they do after time-out.

KEY POINTS TO REMEMBER ABOUT WITHDRAWING REWARDS AND PRIVILEGES

1. Withdraw rewards and privileges during or immediately after the behavior you want to stop.

2. Remove rewards and privileges equal to the misbehavior.

3. Do not take away the same rewards and privileges all the time.

4. When you tell children they are going to lose a reward or privilege, follow through.

5. Do not overuse the withdrawal of rewards and privileges.

6. Continue using the positive skills for desirable behavior.

KEY POINTS TO REMEMBER ABOUT PHYSICAL PUNISHMENT

1. Physical punishment has many negative side effects.
2. Physical punishment should be used for only dangerous or serious behavior.
3. Keep spanking brief but firm.
4. Do not threaten, follow through.
5. Once you decide to punish a behavior physically, do it every time it occurs.
6. Spank only with your open hand on the buttocks.
7. Never spank your children when you are uncontrollably angry.
8. Remember to use the other methods, particularly those that increase behavior.

KEY POINTS TO REMEMBER ABOUT COMPLIANCE

1. Keep requests specific.
2. Make only one request at a time.
3. State requests clearly.
4. State requests only once.
5. Allow a few seconds after a request for children to comply.
6. Respond during or immediately after compliance with praise and attention, rewards and privileges, or suggestive praise.
7. Respond to noncompliance with time-out, removal of rewards and privileges, or spanking.
8. Start with two requests per day and then increase the number.
9. When children comply consistently, make requests more complex.

Appendix C
Mastery Check Forms

Mastery Check Form

Lesson 1: PRAISE and ATTENTION

Criteria:
During the 5-minute Mastery Check, you must give:
5 descriptive praises.

Suggestions:
1. Keep your praises descriptive. For example, instead of saying, "Good boy," say "Good boy. You put all of your toys in the toy box."
2. Use hugs, kisses, and pats on the head with your praises.
3. Praise *during* or *immediately after* good behavior.
4. Remember to praise the small good things your child does.
5. Don't pay attention to minor annoying behavior.

Teaching Child Management Skills

Mastery Check Form

Lesson 2: REWARDS and PRIVILEGES

Criteria:
During the 5-minute Mastery Check, you must give:
2 rewards or privileges.

Suggestions:
1. Use a variety of rewards or privileges. These may be something really special like a new toy or a shopping trip. Or they may be more everyday rewards or privileges like helping mom cook dinner or going for a ride to the store with dad.
2. Be sure to select rewards or privileges that are important to your child.
3. You're already doing many nice things for your children. You cook foods they like, you take them places, you let them watch their favorite TV program instead of yours, you read them stories, and you may even give them an allowance. You can use all of these nice things as rewards and privileges for good behavior.
4. Sometimes, tell your child ahead of time what he must do to earn a reward. Sometimes just surprise him.
5. DO NOT give your child rewards and privileges for *stopping a bad behavior*. This is bribery and it will teach your child to misbehave for **rewards**.

Appendix C

Mastery Check Form

Lesson 3: SUGGESTIVE PRAISE

Criteria:
During the 5-minute Mastery Check you must give:
5 suggestive praises.

Suggestions:
1. Use suggestive praise any time your child is *not* misbehaving or not doing something that has gotten him into trouble before. For example, "Thanks for not being late from school today."

2. Make sure your suggestive praises are sincere. Don't be phony or sarcastic.

3. Keep your suggestive praise descriptive. For example, "Thanks for not putting your wet raincoat on the sofa."

4. If you are using suggestive praise with two children, don't praise one child to make the other child feel bad.

Mastery Check Form

Lesson 4: IGNORING

Criteria:
During the 5-minute Mastery Check, you must give:
0 attention to annoying behavior.

Suggestions:
1. Ignoring means no attention of any kind: no glaring, no staring, no scolding, no explanations, no finger pointing, NO ATTENTION!
2. Don't start to ignore and then give in. This will only teach your child to keep up his misbehavior for a longer period of time.
3. Counting to ten, watching TV, reading, calling a friend, or leaving the room will help you ignore.
4. Always use suggestive praise with ignoring. For example, if you ignore your child's backtalk, the next time he is polite praise him for not backtalking and for being polite.

Appendix C

Mastery Check Form

Lesson 5: TIME-OUT

Criteria:
This Mastery Check has no time limit.
You must.

Use time-out 1 time.

(a) Briefly tell your child what he did wrong.

(b) State that he is to stay in time-out for 3 to 5 minutes.

(c) Ignore any sassing or backtalk.

(d) After his time is up, tell him he may return to play.

Suggestions:
1. Use time-out only for serious behavior problems.
2. When taking your child to the time-out area, be stern and keep your comments brief.
3. Ignore your child's wisecracks or sassing when he is in time-out. Remind him that his time starts when he is quiet.
4. If your child sasses or backtalks when he leaves time-out, return him immediately for another 3 to 5 minutes.
5. Remember to praise him when he is no longer in time-out and is now behaving.

Mastery Check Form

Lesson 6: REMOVING REWARDS and PRIVILEGES

Criteria:
This Mastery Check has no time limit.
You must:

Remove 2 rewards or privileges.
(a) Briefly tell your child what he did wrong.

(b) State that he is to stay in time-out for 3 to 5 minutes.

(c) Ignore any sassing or backtalk.

(d) After his time is up, tell him he may return to play.

Suggestions:
1. Remove rewards and privileges *during* or *immediately after* your child's misbehavior.

2. The privilege you remove should equal the misbehavior of your child.

3. Select a reward or privilege that is important to your child.

4. Follow through: Don't threaten or argue with your child.

Appendix C

Mastery Check Form

Lesson 7: PHYSICAL PUNISHMENT (optional)

Criteria:
This Mastery Check has no time limit.
You must:

Use physical punishment 1 time.

Suggestions:
1. Use physical punishment only for dangerous or extremely serious misbehavior.
2. Be consistent. If you say you're going to punish, follow through.
3. Use physical punishment during or immediately after the problem. Don't delay.
4. Use a brief stern swat with your hand. Don't use objects like hairbrushes, belts or flyswatters.
5. Only spank on the bottom or the hands.
6. Never punish when you're uncontrollably angry.

Teaching Child Management Skills
Mastery Check Form

Lesson 8: COMPLIANCE

Criteria:
This Mastery Check has no time limit.
You must:

(a) Give an instruction to your child. As soon as your child complies, follow through with praise or a reward or privilege.

(b) After you have completed (a), give a second instruction. As soon as your child fails to comply, follow through with time-out or remove a reward or privilege.

Suggestions:
1. Give your instruction clearly so your child hears you, and tell him exactly what you want him to do.
2. After giving an instruction, allow enough time for your child to begin to do what he has been told.
3. Make each request only one time.
4. Ignore complaining.

References

Ayllon, T. & Roberts, M. D. (1975). Mothers as educators for their children. In T. Travis & W. S. Dockens (Eds.), *Applications of Behavior Therapy* (pp. 175–207). New York: Academic Press.

Bach, R. & Moylan, J. J. (1975). Parents administer behavior therapy for inappropriate urination and encopresis: A case study. *Journal of Behavior Therapy and Experimental Psychiatry, 6,* 239–241.

Barlow, D. H. & Hersen, M. (1984). *Single case experimental designs,* second edition. New York: Pergamon.

Becker, W. C. (1960). The relationship of factors in parental rating of self and each other to the behavior of kindergarten children as rated by mothers, fathers, and teachers. *Journal of Consulting Psychology, 24,* 507–527.

Bernal, M. E. (1984). Consumer issues in parent training. In R. F. Dangel & R. A. Polster (Eds.), *Parent Training: Foundations of Research and Practice* (pp. 444–503). New York: Guilford.

Blechman, E. A. (1984). Competent parents, competent children: Behavioral objectives of parent training. In R. F. Dangel & R. A. Polster (Eds.), *Parent Training: Foundations of Research and Practice* (pp. 34–63). New York: Guilford.

Bloom, M. & Fischer, J. (1982). *Evaluating Practice: Guidelines for the accountable professional.* Engelwood Cliffs, N. J: Prentice Hall.

Chilman, C. S. (1975). Programs for disadvantaged parents: Some major trends and related research. In F. D. Horowitz (Ed.), *Review of Child Development Research* (Vol. 4, pp. 215–243). Chicago: University of Chicago Press.

Christophersen, E. R., Barrish, H. H., Barrish I. J. & Christophersen, M. R. (1984). Continuing education for parents of infants and toddlers. In R. F. Dangel & R. A. Polster (Eds.), *Parent Training: Foundations of Research and Practice* (pp. 128–144). New York: Guilford.

Cowen, E. L., Huser, J., Beach, D. R. & Rappaport, J. (1970). Parent perceptions of young children and their relation to indexes of adjustment. *Journal of Consulting and Clinical Psychology, 34,* 97–103.

Dangel, R. F. & Polster, R. A. (Eds.) (1984). *Parent Training: Foundations of Research and Practice.* New York: Guilford.

Dangel, R. F. & Polster, R. A. (1984). WINNING!: A systematic, empirical approach to parent training. In R. F. Dangel & R. A. Polster (Eds.), *Parent Training: Foundations of Research and Practice* (pp. 162–201). New York: Guilford.

Dubey, D. R. & Kaufman, D. F. (1977, August). *Teaching behavior management skills to parents: The group approach.* Paper presented at the 85th Annual Convention of the American Psychological Association, San Francisco. As cited in Gordon, S. B. & Davidson, N. (1981). Behavioral parent training. In A. S. Gurman & D. P. Kniskern (Eds.), *Handbook of*

Family Therapy (pp. 517–555). New York: Brunner/Mazel.
Forehand, R. L. & King, H. E. (1977). Noncompliant children: Effects of parent training on behavior and attitude change. *Behavior Modification, 1,* 93–108.
Forehand, R. L., King, H. E., Peed, S. & Yoder, P. (1975) Mother-child interactions: Comparison of the noncompliant clinic group and a nonclinic group. *Behaviour Research and Therapy. 13,* 79–84.
Forehand, R. L. & McMahon, R. J. (1981). *Helping the Noncompliant Child: A Clinician's Guide to Parent Training.* New York: Guilford.
Gordon, S. B. & Davidson, N. (1981). Behavioral parent training. In A. S. Gurman & D. P. Kniskern (Eds.), *Handbook of Family Therapy* (pp. 517–555). New York: Brunner/Mazel.
Greene, B. F., Clark, H. B. & Risley, T. R. (1977). *Shopping with Children: Advice for Parents.* San Rafael, CA: Academic Therapy Publications.
Hall, M. C. (1984). Responsive parenting: A large-scale training program for school districts, hospitals, and mental health centers. In R. F. Dangel & R. A. Polster (Eds.), *Parent Training: Foundations of Research and Practice* (pp. 67–92). New York: Guilford.
Herbert, E. W. & Baer, D. M. (1972). Training parents as behavior modifiers: self-recording of contingent attention. *Journal of Applied Behavior Analysis, 5,* 139–149.
Holland, C. V. (1969). Elimination by the parents of fire-setting behaviour in a 7-year-old boy. *Behaviour Research and Therapy, 7,* 135–137.
Knight, M. F. & McKenzie, H. S. (1974). Elimination of bedtime thumbsucking in home settings through contingent reading. *Journal of Applied Behavior Analysis, 7,* 33–38.
Leitenberg, H., Burchard, J. D., Burchard, S. N., Fuller, F. J. & Lysaught, T. V. (1977). Using positive reinforcement to suppress behavior: Some experimental comparisons with sibling conflict. *Behavior Therapy, 8,* 168–182.
Lutzker, J. R. (1984). Project 12-ways: Treating child abuse and neglect from an ecobehavioral perspective. In R. F. Dangel & R. A. Polster (Eds.), *Parent Training: Foundations of Research and Practice* (pp. 260–297). New York: Guilford.
McMahon, R. J. & Forehand, R. (1984). Parent training for the noncompliant child: Treatment outcome, generalization, and adjunctive therapy procedures. In R. F. Dangel & R. A. Polster (Eds.), *Parent Training: Foundations of Research and Practice* (pp. 298–328). New York: Guilford.
Neisworth, J. T. & Moore, F. (1972). Operant treatment of asthmatic responding with the parent as therapist. *Behavior Therapy, 3,* 95–99.
Patterson, G. R. (1982). *A social learning approach to family intervention. Vol. 3. Coercive Family Process.* Eugene, OR: Castalia.
Patterson, G. R., Reid, J. B., Jones, R. R. & Conger, R. E. (1975). *A social learning approach to family intervention. Vol. 1. Families with Aggressive Children.* Eugene, OR: Castalia
Pinkston, E. M. (1984). Individualized behavioral intervention for home and school. In R. F. Dangel & R. A. Polster (Eds.), *Parent Training: Foundations of Research and Practice* (pp. 202–238). New York: Guilford.
Pinkston, E. M., Friedman, B. S. & Polster, R. A. (1981). Parents as agents for behavior change. In S. P. Schinke (Ed.) *Behavioral Methods in Social Welfare* (pp. 29–40). New York: Guilford.
Polster, R. A. & Pinkston, E. M. (1979). A delivery system for the treatment of underachievement. *Social Service Review, 53,* 35–55.
Sears, R. R., Macoby, E. & Levin, H. (1957). *Patterns of Child Rearing.* New York: Harper & Row.
Stark, R. & McEvoy, J. (1970). Middle class violence. *Psychology Today, 4,* (6, 107–112). As cited in G. R. Patterson (1982). *A social learning approach to family intervention. Vol. 3. Coercive Family Process.* Eugene, OR: Castalia.
Wahler, R. G. (1969). Oppositional children: A quest for parental reinforcement control. *Journal of Applied Behavior Analysis, 2,* 159–170.

Wahler, R. G. & Dumas, J. E. (1984). Changing the observational coding styles of insular and noninsular mothers: A step toward maintenance of parent training effects. In R. F. Dangel & R. A. Polster (Eds.), *Parent Training: Foundations of Research and Practice* (pp. 379–416). New York: Guilford.

Williams, G. D. (1959). The elimination of tantrum behavior by extinction procedures. *Journal of Abnormal and Social Psychology, 59,* 269–270.

Author Index

Ayllon, T., 29, 149

Bach, R., 29, 149
Baer, D. M., 25
Barlow, D. H. 109, 149
Barrish, H. H. 43, 149
Barrish, I. J. 43, 149
Beach, D. R., 14, 149
Becker, W. C., 14, 149
Bernal, M. E., 103, 149
Blechman, E. A., 103, 149
Bloom, M., 108, 149
Burchard, J. D., 35, 150
Burchard, S. N., 35, 150

Chilman, C. S., 149
Christophersen, E. R., 43, 149
Christophersen, M. R., 43, 149
Clark, H. B., 47, 150
Conger, R. E., 47, 150
Cowen, E. L., 14, 149

Dangel, R. F., vii, 25, 29,35, 149
Davidson, N., 8, 150
Dubey, D. R., 25, 150
Dumas, J. E., 103, 151

Fischer, J., 108, 149
Forehand, R. L., 2, 25, 40, 57, 150

Friedman, B. S., 35, 150
Fuller, F. J., 35, 150

Gordon, S. B., 8, 150
Greene, B. F., 47, 150

Hall, M. C., 29, 40, 150
Herbert, E. W., 25, 150
Hersen, M., 109, 149
Holland, C. V., 47, 150
Huser, J., 14, 149

Jones, R. R., 47, 150

Kaufman, D. F., 25, 149
King, H. E., 25, 150
Knight, M. F., 35, 150

Leitenberg, H., 35, 150
Levin, H., 51, 150
Lutzker, J. R., 2, 150
Lysaught, T. V., 35, 150

Macoby, E., 51, 150
McEvoy, J., 52, 150
McKenzie, H. S., 35, 150
McMahon, R. J., 2, 40, 57, 150

Moore, F., 35, 150
Moylan, J. J., 29, 149

Neisworth, J. T., 35, 150

Patterson, G. R., 47, 52, 57, 150
Peed, S., 150
Pinkston, E. M., 29, 35, 43, 150
Polster, R. A., vii, 25, 29, 35, 150

Rappaport, J., 14, 149

Reid, J. B., 47, 150
Risley, T. R., 47, 150
Roberts, M. D., 29, 149

Sears, R. R., 51, 150
Stark, R., 52, 150

Wahler, R. G., 25, 43, 103, 150, 151
Williams, G. D., 40, 151

Yoder, P., 150

Subject Index

Annoying Habits, 68
Assessment
  of parents, 10
  of the problem, 11
Arguing and Backtalking, 65

Basic Skills
  integrating of, 56
  key points of, 133–139
Becker Bipolar Adjective Checklist, 14
Bedtime, 67
Bedwetting, 69

Causes and Treatment of Childhood Disorders
  assumptions, 4
  changing behavior, 5
  enlisting clients, 8
  parent resistance, 6
Checklists, 14, 114, 118
Child Management Problems
  annoying habits, 68
  arguing and backtalking, 65
  bedtime, 67
  bedwetting, 69
  fighting, 65
  good behavior in public places, 72
  home-school communications, 74
  homework, 73
  household chores, 68
  mealtime, 67
  school problems, 73
  soiling or wetting clothing, 70
  temper tantrums, 66
  using allowances, 76
Collateral Contacts, 116, 118
Commitment, 20
Compliance, 56, 140

Decreasing Inappropriate Behavior, 39
  ignoring, 40
  physical punishment, 51
  time-out, 42
  withdrawing rewards and privileges, 47
Demonstrating Skills, 84
Describing the Service, 17
Direct Observation, 15, 116, 118

Engaging the Parent, 18
Evaluation
  arguments against, 107
  as an ongoing process, 122
  definition, 106
  importance of, 107
  methods, 109
  types of measures, 110
Experimental Designs, 118
  A-B design, 118
  multiple baseline design, 120

Feedback, 85
Fighting, 65

Good Behavior in Public Places, 72
Groups
  arrangements, 80
  composition, 78
  meetings:
    structure and format, 82
    size, 79
    supplies, 81

Home-School Communications, 74
Homework, 73
Household Chores, 68
Hygiene and Appearance, 71

Increasing Appropriate Behavior, 23
  praise and attention, 24
  rewards and privileges, 29
  suggestive praise, 34
Interviewing
  appropriate interviewer behavior, 10
  children, 17
  initial interview, 11

Mealtime, 67

Overview, 2

Parent Attitudes Test, 14
Parent Problems, 93
  drop-outs, 102
  hard-to-reach parents, 104
  in meetings, 93
  in performance, 98
Parent-Trainer Problems, 92
Practice Records, 125–132
Practitioner Behavior, 89

Questionnaires, 115, 118

Resistance
  in parent training, 6
Role-Play, 85, 115, 118

School Problems, 73
Self-Report of Parents, 16, 111, 118
Soiling or Wetting Clothing, 70

Temper Tantrums, 66

Using Allowances, 76

About the Authors

Dr. Richard F. Dangel is a licensed child psychologist and Associate Professor and Chairman, Direct Practice Sequence, Graduate School of Social Work, The University of Texas at Arlington (UTA). He and Dr. Polster co-directed the Parenting Research Station at UTA and developed WINNING!, an empirically based, internationally used, professionally produced, videotaped parenting program. He has authored numerous publications on parenting and the residential care and treatment of children.

Dr. Richard A. Polster is an Associate Professor at The University of Texas at Arlington in the Graduate School of Social Work and serves as a consultant to Human Affairs International, an employee assistance program. Dr. Polster earned his Master's and Ph.D. degrees in social work from the University of Chicago. He has been involved in the research and treatment of children and their families for 17 years. His work is widely published in scholarly journals and books. He is co-editor, with Dr. Dangel, of *Parent Training: Foundations of Research and Practice* (1984), Guilford Press.

Psychology Practitioner Guidebooks

Editors
Arnold P. Goldstein, Syracuse University
Leonard Krasner, Stanford University & SUNY at Stony Brook
Sol. L. Garfield, Washington University

Elsie M. Pinkston & Nathan L. Linsk — CARE OF THE ELDERLY: A Family Approach

Donald Meichenbaum — STRESS INOCULATION TRAINING

Sebastiano Santostefano — COGNITIVE CONTROL THERAPY WITH CHILDREN AND ADOLESCENTS

Lillie Weiss, Melanie Katzman & Sharlene Wolchik — TREATING BULIMIA: A Psychoeducational Approach

Edward B. Blanchard & Frank Andrasik — MANAGEMENT OF CHRONIC HEADACHES: A Psychological Approach

Raymond G. Romanczyk — CLINICAL UTILIZATION OF MICRO-COMPUTER TECHNOLOGY

Philip H. Bornstein & Marcy T. Bornstein — MARITAL THERAPY: A Behavioral-Communications Approach

Michael T. Nietzel & Ronald C. Dillehay — PSYCHOLOGICAL CONSULTATION IN THE COURTROOM

Elizabeth B. Yost, Larry E. Beutler, M. Anne Corbishley & James R. Allender

— GROUP COGNITIVE THERAPY: A Treatment Method for Depressed Older Adults

Lillie Weiss — DREAM ANALYSIS IN PSYCHOTHERAPY

Edward A. Kirby & Liam K. Grimley — UNDERSTANDING AND TREATING ATTENTION DEFICIT DISORDER

Jon Eisenson — LANGUAGE AND SPEECH DISORDERS IN CHILDREN

Eva L. Feindler & Randolph B. Ecton — ADOLESCENT ANGER CONTROL: Cognitive-Behavioral Techniques

Michael C. Roberts — PEDIATRIC PSYCHOLOGY: Psychological Interventions and Strategies for Pediatric Problems

Daniel S. Kirschenbaum, William G. Johnson & Peter M. Stalonas, Jr. — TREATING CHILDHOOD AND ADOLESCENT OBESITY

W. Stewart Agras — EATING DISORDERS: Management of Obesity, Bulimia and Anorexia Nervosa

Ian H. Gotlib & Catherine A. Colby — TREATMENT OF DEPRESSION: An Interpersonal Systems Approach

Walter B. Pryzwansky & Robert N. Wendt — PSYCHOLOGY AS A PROFESSION: Foundations of Practice

Cynthia D. Belar, William W. Deardorff & Karen E. Kelly — THE PRACTICE OF CLINICAL HEALTH PSYCHOLOGY

Paul Karoly & Mark P. Jensen — MULTIMETHOD ASSESSMENT OF CHRONIC PAIN

William L. Golden, E. Thomas Dowd & Fred Friedberg — HYPNOTHERAPY: A Modern Approach

Patricia Lacks — BEHAVIORAL TREATMENT FOR PERSISTENT INSOMNIA

Arnold P. Goldstein & Harold Keller — AGGRESSIVE BEHAVIOR: Assessment and Intervention

C. Eugene Walker, Barbara L. Bonner & Keith L. Kaufman — THE PHYSICALLY AND SEXUALLY ABUSED CHILD: Evaluation and Treatment

Robert E. Becker, Richard G. Heimberg & Alan S. Bellack — SOCIAL SKILLS TRAINING TREATMENT FOR DEPRESSION

Richard F. Dangel & Richard A. Polster — TEACHING CHILD MANAGEMENT SKILLS

Albert Ellis, John F. McInerney, Raymond DiGiuseppe & Raymond Yeager — RATIONAL-EMOTIVE THERAPY WITH ALCOHOLICS AND SUBSTANCE ABUSERS

Johnny L. Matson & Thomas H. Ollendick — ENHANCING CHILDREN'S SOCIAL SKILLS: Assessment and Training